TABLE OF C

D1490733

➤➣•○•➢◄

SECRET		PAGE #

When You Want Something
You Have Never Had,
You Have To Do Something
You Have Never Done.

-MIKE MURDOCK

≈ 1 ≈

The Unforgettable Woman Is Willing To Go Where She Has Never Been To Create Something She Has Never Had

───────≈>•<≈───────

Familiar surroundings are usually comforting, soothing and reassuring.

Some of the largest and most popular restaurant chains have discovered this. One of the greatest hamburger chains in the world has comfortable familiar colors, decor and furniture settings in every single store throughout the world. Their purpose? To make customers feel at ease...at home...comfortable. This enables the customer to sense a friendly atmosphere and climate.

Most women want comfortable circumstances. It is normal to pursue things that are familiar to you.

Comfort can *reduce* the stress of decision-making.

It can *remove* the friction and discomfort of making new friends.

It can make life far easier.

But Ruth is *not* an average woman.

She is an *Unforgettable Woman.*

You see, she knew a truth that most of us never discover—that *comfort can be deteriorating.*

Comfort is death to creativity.

It can destroy potential.

It can neutralize the force called multiplication and increase.

Comfortable people achieve little.

It is *uncomfortable* people who produce miraculous changes in every generation.

It is *uncomfortable* people who *create the currents* that change the very world we live in.

Ruth was willing to *relocate geographically.* She was willing to *disconnect* from her kinfolks. She was willing to go in a direction she had never been and experience discomfort...forfeiting the climate of old friendships in order to birth one of the greatest chapters and beginnings of any generation in history.

Notice the extraordinary champions in the Scriptures who made *geographical changes* that birthed their entry into greatness.

Moses had to leave the comfort of the palace to enter the school of the wilderness.

Daniel was taken into captivity, away from his homeland, for his great gifts to flourish.

Joseph was sold into slavery, away from the comfort of his loving father, Jacob; *then,* he was catapulted and promoted to be prime minister of Egypt.

Abraham had to leave his kinfolks and homeland *before* he tasted the unbelievable blessings of God.

Esther had to be willing to leave those who were raising her when she won the beauty pageant that ushered her in to be queen. As queen, she became the deliverer of an entire nation of people.

Jacob would never have had the incredible experience of the revelation of God near the Jabbok River, until he left the reassuring arms of his mother, Rebekah.

John, the revelator, received his remarkable and supernatural insights *after* he was exiled to the Isle of Patmos.

The *upper room experience* came when 120 people made their way through the streets of Jerusalem into the upper room and received the mighty outpouring of The Holy Spirit, *after* Jesus instructed them to go there.

It was Philip, the Spirit-filled deacon, who was moved out of the great Jerusalem revival and into the desert, where he connected with the Ethiopian eunuch. (Someone has said that 90 percent of Ethiopia was Christianized because of this eunuch's conversion—after God moved a great man.)

Geographical change often positions you to receive supernatural promotion and revelation.

One of the outstanding secrets of *The Unforgettable Woman* is her *willingness to leave the nest.*

She sees something more important than temporary comfort and familiar surroundings.

She knows the rewards of change.

She can *sense* the *benefits beyond the season of difficulty.*

She sees the *end* as clearly as she sees the beginning.

She thinks *ahead.*

She is wise.

Yes, she is unforgettable.

What You Are Willing To Walk Away From Determines What God Will Bring To You.

You may have to disconnect from something you cherish before you ever taste the full and total provision of God during your lifetime.

Zones of thorns...

Chapters of difficulty...

Pages of pain...

Champions are simply those who are willing to make very difficult changes in order to taste the ultimate rewards they are capable of pursuing and reaching.

I have met thousands of people during my lifetime. Conversations continually reveal to me that *mediocrity is merely an attitude,* an unwillingness to make a change.

Incredible jobs await thousands—except it may involve a one hour drive from their house! Rather than move their residence or make the drive, they simply stay and become welded to the seat called mediocrity.

Never Complain About Your Future—If You Are Unwilling To Walk Away From Your Present.

Ruth was willing to pay a price...a *present* penalty...in order to produce an *extraordinary* future. It made her unforgettable.

You See, *Change Is Proof of Trust.*

God's *greatest* need is to be *believed.*

His *only* need is to be believed.

His only *pleasure* is to be believed.

So He continually instructs us to make changes— as proof that we truly trust Him and His authority over our lives.

It will take all the faith you can generate to make

the real changes God requires in your life.

He will *stretch* you.

He will *compel* you.

He will *motivate* you to use every ounce of faith in Him possible. At some point in your life, your *logic* will fail. *Intellect* will fail. *Reasoning* will fail. *Human counsel* will fail.

Yet, you will have to trust somebody.

The marvelous wonder of life is that God truly *can* be trusted. You can trust Him with things you *do not understand.* You can trust Him with a destination that you *do not see clearly.*

Remember Jonah? God had instructed him to "go to Nineveh."

He said, "I would rather go to Tarshish."

Have you been wondering why you are suffocating with seaweed? Did you take off on a cruise and find yourself thrashing through the vomit in the belly-of-a-whale experience? The answer is simple. God scheduled you for Nineveh—and you headed for Tarshish!

If you do not like where you are, maybe you are in the wrong place. (Obviously, you may love where you are and *still* be at the wrong place!)

My telephone rang one day with a brokenhearted pastor at the other end. "Mike, I am desperate. God has just opened a great door for me to pastor, and I have made a decision. My wife is refusing to move with me to the church. She refuses to pray with me over the decision. She says she will never change homes for the rest of her life. What shall I do?"

Obviously, this was not the first problem they had experienced. Without elaborating on possible approaches to help his wife link herself to The Holy Spirit and arrive at an accurate conclusion, let me just say this: This is not a strange story. This happens every single day. Thousands of husbands feel trapped and imprisoned in a marriage that can't really soar, because their wives *refuse to make changes.*

Their careers are sabotaged.

Their enthusiasm is assassinated, simply because someone in the home refuses to make changes.

This was not his first experience with her rebellion. She was sabotaging his calling. He could hardly address the people on Sunday morning. She was a total embarrassment for him in front of his deacon board.

Some would enjoy dissecting the philosophy of the situation. Some would become Job's comforters and tell the minister that her rebellion was for a valid reason. However counselors might choose to handle this, one fact remains clear: *One rebellious mate can fragment the dreams of another through simple unwillingness to make changes.*

Thousands of homes are dashed daily on the rocks of rebellion. Comfort becomes the pursuit instead of the promotion of someone we love.

This tragedy does not happen when you have an Unforgettable Woman in your life.

That's one of the reasons I consider my own mother a truly *Unforgettable Woman.* She had 7 children. My father pioneered small churches throughout the South. The highest salary my father ever received was $125.00 weekly from his church. Yet I never heard my mother complain about him or his following of The Holy Spirit. Changes were often very difficult, but she believed God would honor a submissive spirit.

Your Success Is Always Connected To A Place. If you are not *where* God has assigned you, you will not prosper. Ask Jonah who stands out as a shining example.

Your greatest growth and the greatest chapters of your life were birthed in the climate of discomfort, things that were difficult, things that were uncomfortable.

What You Are Willing
    To Walk Away From
Determines What God
    Will Bring To You.

-MIKE MURDOCK

❧ 2 ❧

THE UNFORGETTABLE WOMAN KNOWS THE SUCCESS OF HER FUTURE DEPENDS ON HER DEPARTURE FROM HER PAST

It fascinates me that Ruth was willing to leave everything comfortable to *pursue her future.* Her kinfolks were in her past. She refused to let her upbringing and her religious background become the noose around her neck that sabotaged her future. She refused to let her past rob her of the potential of tomorrow.

I have said many times that *intolerance of the present creates a future.* As long as you can adapt to the present...you really do not have a future.

Ruth refused to build her future around her past. Some of us remember painful experiences from yesterday. We have built our entire lifestyle around that experience. Our conversations are consumed with occurrences of 10 years ago.

This is dangerous.

It is devastating.

When You Discuss Your Past, You Perpetuate It.

Words impart life. When you continually replay painful confrontations and situations of the past, you are giving life to them, you are giving a future to them.

The Unforgettable Woman permits yesterday to die.

Ruth did. She did not try to straddle the fence. She refused to become the link between the past and her future.

She totally abandoned the empty relationships of her past.

One of the saddest pictures is in the life of the great patriarch, Abraham. He insisted on bringing Lot, his nephew, with him into the future God had prepared. Lot was a distraction. Most of Abraham's continual problems could be traced to the *presence of Lot.* You see, God had told him to leave his kinfolks and move on to a different territory. *He insisted on bringing someone he was comfortable with—to the detriment of his future.*

Yesterday people will rarely enjoy your future.

It is natural and normal to want to bring everyone close to us into the chapters of our future success. Few will qualify.

Your future must be *earned.*

It is *not* guaranteed. It is *not* the same for everyone. Your future is a Harvest produced by the Seeds you are willing to sow. Bringing yesterday people into the future is like using old wineskins for the new wine of tomorrow. It simply will not work.

So, *prepare to enter your future without yesterday people.* God will bring the right associations with you...or He has scheduled outstanding Divine connections beyond your greatest and wildest dreams.

Move away from yesterday. You have exhausted its benefits. Refuse to waste your energy on repairing it. Rather, rebuild by focusing on your future. Certainly, yesterday can be a reservoir of Wisdom and information. You are not forfeiting loyalty. You are not forgetting the precious lives whom God used mightily for your continual survival and success. But you are refusing to abort your future joys and victories by replaying the memories of yesterday's painful experiences.

Paul refused to wallow in the tears of his past. Few made greater mistakes than he. He caused people to be cast into prison. Christians were murdered because of him. He held the coats of those who stoned the great deacon, Stephen. Yet he refused to forfeit his future by focusing on his past.

His mistakes were *over.*

His sins were *behind* him.

His name had been *changed.*

Eventually, you will be forced to make a major decision in your life. *It will be the decision to totally abandon your memories, and empty your energy into the palace of your future.*

Your conversation must become more creative. Start using your imagination instead of your memories. Meet new friends. Experience new places.

Ruth knew when she had exhausted the benefits of her present season. This is so powerful and important. Every season in your life contains certain advantages. Whether it is one month of a relationship or 90 days on a job, you must discern the Divine purposes of God in *every situation* in your life. You must discern the Divine purpose of God in *every relationship.*

Never linger in a conversation with someone when it is over. Would you keep chewing the same mouthful of food for 3 hours? Of course not. Would you keep reading the same page of a book for 3 days? Of course not. Would you leave a broken record on at the same groove replaying the same note over and over again for several hours? Of course not. Would you keep brushing your teeth for 12 hours in a row? Of course not.

When something is finished, it is finished.

Discern it. Recognize it. Look for it. Consistently be intuitive and discerning when a specific season in your life has *concluded.* Then, move *quickly* and *expectantly* to the next season God has arranged for you.

This quality made Ruth unforgettable.

3

The Unforgettable Woman Knows Exactly What She Wants

Ruth was *decisive*. Few people are.

Have you ever noticed the hesitation in car drivers at a 4-way stop? I have seen people sit for 30 seconds at a 4-way stop waiting for everyone else to make the first move! I have sat at restaurants with people who could not decide in 20 minutes what food they wanted to eat! Some have even asked the waitress what *she* thought they should eat!

Develop decisiveness. Think about what you want. Give it thought. Invest the Seed of time. Contemplate. *Meditate on it.*

What do you want to be happening in the circle of your life *10 years from today?* What are the *ideal* circumstances for your retirement? *What do you dream of becoming?* Do you have a personal list of goals and dreams? Have you taken the time to *write them out in detail?*

Several years ago a brilliant young lady suggested that I take a tape recorder, walk into each room of my home and describe clearly what I wished that room to look like. Something wonderful happened! I described exactly how many pens and pencils I wanted, the kind of paper I wanted beside the telephone, and so forth. It became elaborate, energizing and thrilling.

Few people have taken the time to find out what really excites them, energizes them and motivates them.

Something interesting happened in my personal meditation time some weeks ago. I had been a little concerned that my interests frequently changed. For example, the colors my decorator would select for my home would be exciting and thrilling to me. I felt that I would never want to change my mind about them for years to come. A few weeks later, I discovered another combination of colors that excited me again. Obviously, I did not feel comfortable about suddenly changing everything that had been done in my home. Nor did I really have the finances to do so. I bought a car. Loved it...for about 3 weeks. Then, I was bored and wanted to change.

I felt impressed of The Holy Spirit to begin to write down a list of the things that had *never changed* inside me over many years. It was quite a list of interesting things...and it really put my mind at ease that there was more stability within me than I realized. Many things have *never* changed whatsoever within me, such as my love for information, my desire to collect books and my excitement over receiving a new rare coin from a friend. Another thing that has never changed is my continual need to change my environment. Regardless of how beautifully my bedroom or kitchen were done... within 12 months or so, I was tired of it. That has been consistent.

Some things never change about you. What are they? Put this book down for about 15 minutes. Take a sheet of paper, and as quickly and thoroughly as possible, begin to document the things about yourself that have been pretty consistent over the years. Go ahead. Do it *now*.

Now, after you have done this, you will begin to get a fairly accurate and specific photograph of certain things that you want to be in your life and around you *daily*. You will also get an awareness of the *quality* of life you are struggling to experience.

Some years ago, I asked a consultant to come into my offices for several days. He was to discuss any complaints or ideas with each of my staff. Then I wanted him to compile a report, unbiased and unprejudiced, as to what he thought about our ministry organization. He interrogated me and questioned me for hours. He would take long walks with me and ride in the car; even while I was in crusades, we would talk on the phone. His constant questioning sharpened my focus remarkably. I have never forgotten it.

He was relentless in collecting data about my personal needs, desires and appetites toward life. When were the *happiest* moments of my life? What days did I seem to enjoy life *more* than usual? What were the 3 biggest problems I thought about *the most* every day? Who were the people that were stressful for me to be around? Who were the people in whose presence I was the most relaxed? How did I want to be remembered? What did I consider to be the most important task that I did each day? Weekly? Monthly? If I had to eliminate 50 percent of my entire ministry workload, what would I *delete?* If I were to have a sudden health crisis, experiencing a heart attack or some other medical emergency, what would I change *first* about my *daily lifestyle?*

Riveting questions were hurled at me continually. Slowly but surely, a remarkable understanding of what I *really* wanted out of life developed.

Here is a marvelous little exercise. It could change your life forever. Ask one or two of your closest friends, who are skilled at analyzing and dissecting situations, to interrogate you—quizzing you relentlessly, extracting information from you until you have a perfect and complete photograph of the invisible future *you are laboring to bring to reality.* Something is driving you, pushing you and forcing you toward your future. *What is the invisible dream you are subconsciously trying to birth within you and your life?*

Decisiveness is magnetic.

It is the catalyst for the aura that surrounds extraordinary and unforgettable people. *They simply know exactly what they want.*

When you are sitting in a restaurant sometime, do a little test. Carefully observe the entry of customers. Notice those who saunter and amble in as if they are not quite certain they have chosen the right restaurant. They slowly walk to their seats wondering if they should even stay at the restaurant, or should they select a different table? Then, observe carefully those who stride in confidently and with a firm, clear and raised voice express to the hostess of the restaurant, "Good evening! We need a table for 4—by the window, if possible!" Notice how the hostess responds quickly, with enthusiasm, and immediately begins to communicate to the other workers exactly what was requested.

When ordering your own meal at a restaurant,

speak up. Speak firmly. Don't mumble.

Someone has said, "If you will raise your voice 10 percent and walk 20 percent faster, you will generate remarkable new energy, compelling others to respond favorably to you and raising the level of self-confidence in every single person around you."

James 1:6-8 says, "But let him ask in faith, nothing wavering. For he that wavereth is like a wave of the sea driven with the wind and tossed. For let not that man think that he shall receive anything of the Lord. A double minded man is unstable in all his ways."

What happens when you are totally undecided about an issue or decision? There's a reason for it. It may be lack of *sufficient* information. It may be lack of *accurate* information. When that happens, simply declare with great decisiveness, "I have decided to wait 90 days until additional information arrives." You have retained the climate of confidence and decisiveness. Make decisions clearly.

Notice Ruth said it quite clearly, "Whither thou goest, I will go; and where thou lodgest, I will lodge," (Ruth 1:16).

She knew what she wanted. She *communicated* to Naomi what she wanted. She was bold about *what she wanted.*

It made her unforgettable.

You Will Only Possess
What You Are
Willing To Pursue.

-MIKE MURDOCK

⮞ 4 ⮜

The Unforgettable Woman Is Bold About Her Desires And Communicates Them Clearly To Others

Boldness Has Power.

Ruth had stopped pursuing suggestions from others. Her decision had already been made. She knew what she wanted. Nobody else had discerned her heart. Her sister-in-law had not caught on. Naomi, her experienced mother-in-law, had not perceived it.

So Ruth proceeded to *inform* them.

Read Ruth 1:16-18 very carefully and you will see a *made-up mind.* "And Ruth said, Intreat me not to leave thee, or to return from following after thee: for whither thou goest, I will go; and where thou lodgest, I will lodge: thy people shall be my people, and thy God my God: Where thou diest, will I die, and there will I be buried: the Lord do so to me, and more also, if ought but death part thee and me. When she saw that she was stedfastly minded to go with her, then she left speaking unto her."

You never forget a woman like this.

She was not double-minded. You did not have to wonder about the *direction* she was going. There was no doubt about her *desire.* She was not wasting her time hoping, hinting or asking subtle questions.

Now, this is *not* the ostentatious and brash boldness of a street prostitute.

This is *not* the inexperienced fumblings of a child grappling with the future.

This is a grown and mature widow who now takes charge of her turf by declaring boldly that she is going to follow her mother-in-law her entire lifetime and even unto her death.

This is the kind of woman America desperately needs today.

Thousands change their minds within 60 seconds. This explains the tragedy of millions of broken homes. It explains how the breakdown of conversation has become epidemic in America. Millions of couples stare sullenly at TV screens, while volcanoes of desires within them remain unexpressed and unreleased. These needs, appetites and desires become raging infernos, until one day they explode unharnessed and without control, destroying instead of bonding people together.

The Chief of Staff of one of our late presidents made an interesting comment. Someone asked him how he was so successful in coordinating the diverse personalities and complex tasks which he supervised. He said, "I manage by the acorn philosophy. As soon as I detect a potential problem birthing, I refuse to wait until it becomes an oak tree. I deal with it while it is in the acorn stage."

What are your *exact expectations* of your mate? Of your children? Of your employees? Do *they* know exactly what your needs are? Have you clearly and articulately expressed those needs to *them?* But, you ask indignantly, "What if they have never pursued that understanding of me? Suppose my mate has never asked me my opinion on an issue or what I want?"

If this is the case, it is your personal responsibility to educate those around you regarding your personal needs, desires and appetites.

Obviously, *timing* is important. *Listening* to their needs as well is your personal responsibility also. Providing them a forum in which to express opposing feelings *is a gift you can give to them* as well. "Be kindly affectioned one to another with brotherly love; in honour preferring one another," (Romans 12:10).

It will make you unforgettable to others.

Everything God Created Is A Solution To A Problem.

-MIKE MURDOCK

≋ 5 ≋

THE UNFORGETTABLE WOMAN KNOWS TO WHOM SHE HAS BEEN ASSIGNED

Everything God Has Created Is To Solve A Problem.

That's the purpose of any creation. Every inventor knows this.

Creativity is merely the solution to current problems.

Mechanics solve automobile problems.

Accountants solve tax problems.

Lawyers solve legal problems.

Mothers solve emotional problems.

Ministers solve spiritual problems.

You were created to solve some kind of problem while you are on earth.

Your Assignment is always to a specific person or to a group of people. Moses' Assignment was to the Israelites. Aaron's Assignment was to Moses.

Your Assignment is always to enable someone to succeed in some area of their life.

Ruth knew her Assignment was specifically to Naomi. She uncluttered her life of any options. Alternatives were not considered. She severed commitments to every other human on earth. She abandoned herself totally to the survival and success of her widowed mother-in-law.

Focus is very powerful. It is magnetic. It is the mysterious secret behind the invisible current called power.

You will only succeed with something that consumes you.

It is the reason many homes have crumbled. The focus has been broken. Many wives are more excited over their boss and job than their husband and children. Many husbands have forgotten to be the priest of their home and the protector of their wives. Consumed with their pursuit of financial success or fame in the business world, they have forgotten to whom they have been assigned.

Someone is supposed to succeed *because of you.* *Who is it?*

Someone will fail unless your attention is wholly upon them. Who is it?

It astounds me that thousands have no real concern about their place of employment—it is merely a paycheck. It seems their paycheck is of greater priority than the person for whose success they are responsible.

It is a forever memory in my mind. I had finished preaching one night at a great conference here in Dallas, Texas. A very sharp looking young lady had been sitting on the front seat the entire service. She approached me after the service. Her eyes were on fire. Excitement was written all over her countenance.

"I am going to work for you. Somehow... someday...soon. I know I am assigned to you. God told me that tonight." She was very energized as she spoke.

I smiled and said rather quietly, "That's wonderful. I am sure God will direct your steps."

A few weeks later, I walked in my office after flying in from a great crusade. There she was in my office. She had been hired by my office manager as his personal secretary. She seemed vivacious, alive and very enthusiastic. A few weeks later she approached me, and said, "I still feel I am *assigned to you.* Whenever your secretary leaves, I want to apply for that position."

Some weeks later it happened, and I hired her. Within 60 days, she had a fresh and *different* revelation. The pressure was too great. The stress was too continual. When I arrived home from a crusade, she had resigned suddenly, and I did not see her again for a long time. Obviously, she was not really persuaded about her Assignment.

Your Assignment may not appear too appealing initially. I am certain that assisting an elderly widow who was impoverished and broken was not exactly an exciting venture. But Ruth knew to whom she had been assigned. *Nothing else mattered.*

God created Moses to be a deliverer...to enable the Israelites to move out of captivity.

He created Aaron to hold up the hands of Moses.

He created David to break the tyranny of Saul who was leading Israel into a backslidden state.

He created Jonathan to honor and strengthen David in preparation for kingship.

He created Joseph to make Pharaoh successful and to enable his own family to survive a terrible famine.

Whose success really matters to you?

Whose *failure* would cause you to ache and agonize inside?

Whose pain do you feel?

You may be called to pour healing oil on the broken

heart of a battered wife. Injustice may infuriate you, or maybe God has called you to open a home for abused children.

Whatever it is—give yourself totally to your Assignment. It is *only* when you are consumed with another person's success that your own success will emerge.

Is your elderly mother's home neglected and unkept? Do you live a mere hour away? Go to her home. Invest a day of your energy and time. Encourage her, and ease her burden.

Find Your Assignment.

You see, when you are assigned to someone, everything that happens to them *matters to you.* Everything that hurts them...hurts *you.* Everything that brings them joy...brings *you* joy.

Ruth knew when her Assignment had changed.

Few do. Many husbands cannot get away from mother's apron strings and continue to show divided loyalties. Many wives keep telephoning home and want to go back home for "awhile." "Therefore shall a man leave his father and his mother, and shall cleave unto his wife: and they shall be one flesh," (Genesis 2:24).

Your Assignment can change. For a long season of her life, Naomi was Ruth's Assignment. But when Boaz entered her life, the seasons changed. She did not forsake Naomi, but her devotion to Naomi was a model and monument in the mind of Boaz of what her loyalty to him would be like.

Discern when your Assignment has changed.

⟩⟩ 6 ⟨⟨

The Unforgettable Woman Makes Her Assignment An Obsession

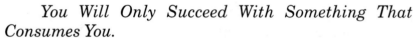

You Will Only Succeed With Something That Consumes You.

Significant achievers build their *daily agenda* around their Assignment. Their schedule and their plan is totally focused on the completion of their Assignment. Their library is filled with books...about *their Assignment.* Their best friends are those who *celebrate* (not tolerate) *their Assignment.*

When you hear the name of Thomas Edison, you think of inventions. When you hear the name of Oral Roberts, you think of healing. When you hear the name of Henry Ford, you think of an automobile. When you hear the name of Michael Jordan, you think of basketball.

You Will Only Be Remembered For Your Obsession In Life. It may be a good one or an evil one. Whether you are Billy Graham or Adolph Hitler—you will be known for one thing: *what consumes you,* your mind and your time.

Ruth would not even pursue the normal path of dating others. She built her lifestyle around the survival of Naomi. *She never considered an option.*

It may be your personal *business.* It may be the spiritual life of your *children. You will almost always succeed with anything that has the ability to demand your total focus and attention.*

Joshua called it "not looking to the right or the left." Others call it being single-minded. "A double minded man is unstable in all his ways," (James 1:8).

She refused to consider any alternatives to her Assignment. Ruth would not go back to her in-laws. She refused to return to the village of her youth. She had developed total focus on her Assignment.

The Only Reason Men Fail Is Broken Focus. If you fail in life...it will be because something was introduced to you as an option, an alternative to what God told you to do with your life, and *you accepted it.*

Look at Moses. "When he was come to years, refused to be called the son of Pharaoh's daughter; Choosing rather to suffer affliction with the people of God, than to enjoy the pleasures of sin for a season; Esteeming the reproach of Christ greater riches than the treasures in Egypt: for he had respect unto the recompence of the reward," (Hebrews 11:24-26).

There is no Plan B for your life. There is only one plan. It is the master plan of the Creator Who made you. Consider nothing else as an option.

That's what made Ruth an *Unforgettable Woman.*

≈ 7 ≈

THE UNFORGETTABLE WOMAN EMBRACES HER ASSIGNMENT WITHOUT ANYONE TO ENCOURAGE HER

As Naomi walked with her two daughters-in-law, Orpah and Ruth, she turns and says, "Go, return each to her mother's house: the Lord deal kindly with you, as ye have dealt with the dead, and with me. The Lord grant you that ye may find rest, each of you in the house of her husband," (Ruth 1:8-9). She kissed them. They wept.

Both said, "We will return with thee unto thy people."

Naomi instructed, "Turn again, my daughters: why will ye go with me? Are there yet any more sons in my womb, that they may be your husbands? Turn again, my daughters, go your way; for I am too old to have an husband," (Ruth 1:11-12).

They lifted up their voice.

They wept again.

Orpah left.

But Ruth cleaved unto her.

Naomi rebukes, "Behold, thy sister in law is gone

back unto her people, and unto her gods: return thou after thy sister in law," (Ruth 1:15).

Ruth is *tenacious.*

She is *bold.*

She is *focused.*

Her husband is dead.

Her father-in-law is dead.

Her sister-in-law has returned to her family.

Her mother-in-law is instructing her to return home.

There is not one encourager in her circle. She does not have one single spiritual cheerleader in her life.

She is *alone.*

She is the only one with the desire to pursue a different future.

Her past has no encouraging memories.

Her present has no encouraging motivation.

Her future is up to her alone.

She knows it.

"Intreat me not to leave thee, or to return from following after thee: for whither thou goest, I will go; and where thou lodgest, I will lodge: thy people shall be my people, and thy God my God: Where thou diest, will I die, and there will I be buried: the Lord do so to me, and more also, if ought but death part thee and me," (Ruth 1:16-17).

She was willing to motivate herself when nobody else was capable or caring.

Most of us appreciate a lot of encouragement. Daily. Consistently. It is wonderful when your mate is there to hold your hand through the valleys of uncertainty. It is a precious thing when your little girl looks up and says, "Daddy, you can do anything!"

Your pastor is a gift from the Lord when he looks into your eyes and tells you, "I prayed for you last night, and God spoke to me to reassure you and tell you that your circumstances are going to change very soon."

But what if there were no one in your life to speak a word to encourage you? Would you *still* persist in the way you are going? Would you *stay* focused? Would you remain bold and *tenacious* in your goal and dream—when absolutely nobody *really* cared?

That is what made Ruth an *Unforgettable Woman.*

It is what can make you an unforgettable champion right now.

You see, *every true champion knows seasons of aloneness.* Moses must have known *seasons of insignificance* alone in the desert. David must have felt disconnected from the great climate his brothers enjoyed, as they won victory after victory in Saul's army. Certainly, it is wonderful and desirable to have encouragement around you. But if you are really going to produce significantly, you must learn the secret of *motivating yourself...encouraging* yourself...accessing the deepest currents within your own heart.

If you keep waiting for everyone else—you will never move from where you are.

You can *stay* motivated.

You can *stay* enthusiastic.

You can *stay* energized.

You can motivate yourself—when you develop a consuming obsession for a specific future you desire.

So stop complaining that your mate is not interested in your personal dreams.

Stop whining when your children show no interest in your personal goals.

Stop holding self-pity parties. Nobody attends them anyhow.

Embrace your future. Do it with total abandonment, joy and full excitement that *tomorrow is going to be the best season of your life.*

Any Assignment From God
Will Benefit
Someone Else
Besides Yourself.

-*MIKE MURDOCK*

⤳ 8 ⤳

THE UNFORGETTABLE WOMAN FOCUSES COMPLETELY ON THE SUCCESS OF SOMEONE ELSE

Ruth declared total allegiance and loyalty to Naomi.

The success and well being of Naomi mattered to her more than anything else. Read Ruth 1:16-17 again and again throughout this book, and you will see that she was consumed with being a companion, devoted protégé and follower of her mother-in-law.

My life was radically changed many years ago at 2:30 one morning. It was the concluding day of a 5-day fast. At that time, my office was my little garage in Houston, Texas. As I was praying fervently for God to touch my life and multiply my success, He spoke a single sentence that became the motto of my life: *"What You Make Happen For Others, I Will Make Happen For You."* At first, I thought The Holy Spirit was simply repeating to my spirit a very common statement heard my entire life. It was the golden rule of Jesus. "Therefore all things whatsoever ye would that men should do to you, do ye even so to them: for this is the law and the prophets."

So, I simply replied to God as He spoke to my heart, "I *know* that if I treat someone good, they will treat me good."

"I did not say that."

Again, the Lord spoke to my heart so clearly, "*What You Make Happen For Others—I Will Make Happen For You.*" It was then that something exploded in my spirit. You see, we have been taught our entire lives that if we treat someone kindly, they will be kind to us. How ridiculous! You know better than that already, don't you? Think of someone you have treated very well who turned on you and bit you like a mad dog.

Jesus simply said to treat others with the same respect and love that we would want someone to treat us. He never promised that those you treated kindly would respond identically. What God did say was, "With good will doing service, as to the Lord, and not to men: *Knowing that whatsoever good thing any man doeth, the same shall he receive of the Lord,* whether he be bond or free," (Ephesians 6:7-8).

When you treat someone right, God will schedule someone into your life to treat *you* well. That is His promise. Is there a major difference? Incredibly so.

You see, when you do someone "*a favor,*" it often intimidates them and makes them feel like they now owe you a return favor. This is bribery. This is obligatory. This destroys true friendship. Why? *You will always resent someone you owe.* Also, when you do someone a favor, you are now limited to their ability to return it—and also limited to *the schedule* that they decide to perform it for you.

However, when you show "favor" toward

somebody—then, God has guaranteed He will send someone else on His schedule—with His ability to bless you in return. God becomes the Lord of the Harvest *instead* of the person who received your good deed.

When Job prayed for his friends, his own captivity was turned. "And the Lord turned the captivity of Job, when he prayed for his friends; also the Lord gave Job twice as much as he had before," (Job 42:10).

When Abraham decided to forfeit his right to beautiful land in order to secure peace with Lot, God spoke 4 verses later: "And the Lord said unto Abram, after that Lot was separated from him, Lift up now thine eyes, and look for the place where thou art northward, and southward, and eastward, and westward: *For all the land which thou seest, to thee will I give it, and to thy seed for ever.* And I will make thy seed as the dust of the earth: so that if a man can number the dust of the earth, then shall thy seed also be numbered. Arise, walk through the land in the length of it and in the breadth of it; for I will give it unto thee," (Genesis 13:14-17). *When Abraham concentrated on his nephew Lot's success, God got involved with his success.*

Joseph concentrated on the success of Potiphar, and God blessed him. He interpreted the dream of the butler and experienced a dramatic promotion 24 months later.

Any Assignment From God Will Benefit Someone Else Besides Yourself. It is important for you to totally focus on helping someone else reach their dreams and goals. It is vital. It is absolutely necessary. *Someone should succeed because of your life.* Who is it?

Ruth was unforgettable because she discovered this secret.

Greatness Is
Simply Fulfilling
God's Expectations
of You.

-MIKE MURDOCK

⇒ 9 ⇐

The Unforgettable Woman Knows Greatness When She Gets In The Presence of It

Ruth was the daughter-in-law of Naomi. She had observed this old and experienced mother of Israel closely for a number of years. She was married to Naomi's son, and had observed in her mother-in-law a profound understanding of life and men.

She saw greatness in a woman much older than herself.

You have often observed the ignorance of the young. I heard a teenager sneer at his parent some weeks ago, as if the parent knew nothing about life. The teenage boy couldn't even make enough money to buy his own food, much less his car or house. But in the folly of his youth, he never discerned the remarkable accomplishments of his mother and father. (Of course, I remember the same ignorant season in my youth— and this gives me patience with them!)

Unfortunately, some never grow up. Many never learn that *greatness is not always easily discerned.*

Some of the most remarkable people on earth may be in your own household, and you never discover it.

Look at Joseph. He had dreams. He could interpret them. He knew their value. He saw greatness in discerning the future. He was articulate in his description. He had the integrity, honesty and openness to share it with his own brothers. *Yet his own brothers never sensed that destiny was on the head of their baby brother. Joseph was the master key to their future survival.* He was the only reason they would have a future. He would provide for their father in his old age. His Wisdom would be pursued by the Pharaoh of Egypt. He would design the food plan for millions of people.

Yet his own brothers never grasped it.

Begin with your own family. Each one of them contains something extraordinary. *What is it?* What are their greatest gifts, skills or talents? What traits and characteristics are worth observing? *Have others discerned something in them that you have not?*

Observe those on your job. Someone in your office has seen something you have never seen. They contain information you have not yet tapped into. *What is it?*

Look twice at the mentors who are crossing your life. What have they accomplished? What battles have they won? What hurdles have they jumped? What difficult rivers have they crossed? What mountains have they tunneled through? *They have survived. How?*

Interrogate. Interview. Extract information from their lives.

What *financial* devastation have they tasted and overcome? What *false accusations* have been hurled, and yet they withstood them? What *misunderstandings* have occurred, and yet they kept their focus? What *traps* have they miraculously avoided?

Every mentor *has defeated a different enemy.*

Every mentor uses *different weaponry.*

Every mentor has a *different focus.*

Discern greatness wherever you find it. One evening at supper a close friend of mine paid the food ticket for a man across the restaurant. He did it quietly and without fanfare and then explained to me: "He is tremendous in the field of sports. He has overcome great odds. He's quite a famous man in baseball. I always honor greatness in any field—in any way that I can." He then mentioned that he will often write a note of gratitude to someone that has achieved something of significance, even when they have never met him. It is his way of *honoring greatness.*

Look at King Saul. He was a very foolish man in many ways. But he had enough sense to know when the mantle of greatness was on a shepherd boy. He knew that it was more than a miracle slingshot that brought Goliath down. He quickly perceived that a supernatural hand was upon the shoulder of the young shepherd. He saw the power of his music. It did not take him long to discover satanic spirits were uncomfortable when David played the harp. Even King Saul *pursued* greatness, when he felt inferior to everything around him.

Elisha knew greatness when he got in the presence of it. This is why he asked Elijah to let him stay by his side and reap the benefits of that mantle of anointing.

Joshua knew greatness when he got in the presence of it. That's why he called Moses the servant of the Lord and followed his instructions even when it was contrary to his own heart.

Another uncommon woman was Abigail. When her fool husband, Nabal, refused to recognize the greatness of the future king of Israel, David, she went the extra mile. She pursued David and provided the food necessary for him and his men.

Make it a habit to speak with genuine awareness and respect to anyone who has attained a measure of greatness.

Greatness is often camouflaged. Few discern it. It is often buried under the tattered garments of humanity, personality quirks and opposing opinions.

When Ruth got in the presence of Naomi, she was quite aware that this embittered, broken and lonely woman of God contained an invisible force. This was the magnet that helped her sever her ties with her heathenistic family.

You see, Jesus was around many people who never discerned that He was even a healer. But those who discerned it received incredible miracles.

One of the greatest evangelists that God ever placed in Christianity told me something interesting one day. He related how he had often been in the presence of young ministers who had just entered their ministry. During two hour lunches or times together, not one question was ever asked him relating to the healing river of ministry that flowed through him and how to make it happen in *their* own ministry and lives.

If there is any cry that ought to erupt from our hearts during these days, it should be the cry for God to give us *the ability to recognize greatness when we get in the presence of it.* Ask God to forgive you for overlooking those who have paid dearly for the mantle wrapped around their lives. How sad to live around it, next to it, sit at the table with it...and never drop your pail into the Well of Living Water that God has so generously placed within the hearts and minds of those around you.

Some of the greatest people on earth are not always *noticeably* great.

Paul said that when he was with people, he *appeared* weak. He knew that it was *not* his presence that made an impression. (Maybe that's why he had to write so many letters—people didn't enjoy his presence as much as his letters!) Seriously, he was very sharp, persuasive and capable. However, *God's gold bars do not always arrive wrapped in silk and satin.* They often come wrapped in burlap or even brown paper sacks. Their wrappings may not be fancy.

Your mentors are not necessarily magnetic. They are not always persuasive and dynamic. Take time to notice that *others see things you have never seen.* They know what you have never discovered. They sense what you have never felt.

Discern greatness, and you too will become unforgettable.

Uncommon People
Will Ignite
The Uncommon
In You.

-MIKE MURDOCK

❧ 10 ❧

THE UNFORGETTABLE WOMAN IS WILLING TO PAY ANY PRICE NECESSARY TO STAY IN THE PRESENCE OF AN EXTRAORDINARY PERSON

Several years ago, a young lady working for me informed me that a dear friend of mine was coming through town on a particular Tuesday. He had telephoned to have lunch with me.

"Great!" I was enthusiastic.

"Oh, but that is not possible," she explained. "I told him you could not make the luncheon date because your flight was leaving during that time."

"Simply change the flight for two or 3 hours later," I explained.

"But that would cost an extra $500 to make any change on your ticket," she replied rather exasperated.

"Make the changes anyway," I explained patiently. "You see, I realize that $500 is a lot of money. But it is a very small price to pay to get to have lunch with this particular friend. He is probably the wisest man I know in certain fields. When he talks to me, creativity bursts in me like Niagara Falls. My greatest ideas often come *when I am in his presence.* He teaches me what no one else teaches me. No human has ever spoken to me the things this man speaks into my life. No, make the necessary changes and I will forfeit the $500 *because I can always replace money—but I cannot replace the Wisdom that is imparted from this man.*"

I'm still not sure whether she ever quite understood me, but I am certain of this: Exceptional and extraordinary people must be *pursued.*

That's why the little woman with the issue of blood was willing to crawl through the crowd to touch the hem of the garment of Christ. *She was willing to pay any price to connect with Someone more powerful than herself.*

Elisha pursued Elijah. *He understood the reward system.* He wanted a double portion of the miracle mantle that was on the prophet Elijah. He knew that it would *not* come in the normal, ordinary routine of things. Supernatural things do not just happen. *Promotions are not accidents.*

I am persuaded that extraordinary people are always just beyond your reach. They are not always accessible to everyone, easy to reach or easy to connect with.

It may be *gold* inside the bank vault.

It may be *diamonds* in the depths of the earth.

It may be *people* who know the secrets of life.

If you ever draw water from the deepest wells on earth, you're going to have to bring your own bucket, drop your own rope and take the time to draw the water.

I was speaking in a great church in Phoenix, Arizona, when a lady approached me afterward. As she explained her problem, I simply referred her to a book on my book table that contained the answer.

"Oh, I never have paid that much for a book," she exclaimed.

"Have you ever paid that much for a meal?" I asked.

"Oh, yes, of course!" she answered.

"In other words, you are telling me that your waistline excites you more than your mind," I teased.

It is quite puzzling and fascinating to me. We will pay $20,000 for an automobile that never talks to us, nor gives us one piece of information, nor radically changes our life. Yet we will stand and argue with the bookstore manager over a $10 book that contains 20 years of research.

I purchased a book one day for $84. One single book—for $84. A young man with me was shocked.

"I cannot believe that you would pay $84 for a single book!" he said, stunned.

"I did not pay $84 for a book in reality," I replied. "It took this author 20 years of constant research to discover truths that I will know within two hours. I would be an absolute fool to refuse to hand him $84 for working to find the answers I have wanted. Actually, it's impossible to find anyone who will work 20 years for you for a mere $84."

Authors are your research assistants.

I have invested thousands of hours of research, poured over huge stacks of material, toiled all hours of the night...to place in a single book the greatest secrets on earth. Then, I have watched husbands and wives argue with each other at the book table as to whether or not they should pay $10 for that research.

The ignorant are always so obvious. It may be difficult to discern the intelligent, but it's never difficult to discern the ignorant.

I read an interesting story a few days ago in one of

the success magazines. A young entrepreneur desperately wanted to meet a famous man. He wanted a mentor. He wanted advice and desperately wanted access to this man. It seemed utterly impossible. He wrote letters. He telephoned. Nothing seemed to break through the wall that *protected the focus* of the great achiever.

He finally found out the favorite restaurant where the man loved to eat and waited for hours. *Contact* was made. The relationship was birthed. But it *cost him* time and effort.

Ruth was not an average woman.

She received not one single word of encouragement from her sister-in-law, Orpah.

She received no encouragement from her kinfolks she was leaving.

She received no encouragement from her husband, because he was dead.

She received no encouragement from Naomi, the very mentor she was pursuing.

In fact, there is not one single sentence in the Bible that indicates she received any encouragement whatsoever to make the geographical changes she made.

Yet she honored what her heart discerned.

She celebrated greatness in another.

She knew the key to changing her seasons was linked to *staying* in the presence of Naomi.

Unforgettable people invest more energy in their pursuits.

It may take 20 phone calls instead of one.

It may take 10 letters instead of two.

It may take working an extra 4 hours instead of 10 minutes overtime.

It may require taking a lower salary for a year

instead of a higher salary.

Every price tag is different, but you can believe anything of value has a price.

Why is it worth it to pursue the climate or atmosphere of an extraordinary person?

Their *aura* will *energize* you.

Their *expectations* will *stretch* you.

Their *impatience* will *quicken* you.

Their *focus* will *remind* you.

Their *weaknesses* will even *encourage* you. (When you observe their flaws in the midst of their great productivity, it will encourage you that you too—with your own flaws—can achieve great heights of accomplishment!)

Their *creativity* will unleash waves of new *ideas* within you.

Their *failures* will *enlighten* you.

Your best will come out of you in the presence of extraordinary people.

Your worst ideas will be exposed and wither in their presence.

As I review my own life, I recall with great and deep gratitude the moments I have been exposed to remarkable champions in my generation. Their focus was almost unbelievable. *Their unwillingness to engage in trivia intrigued me.* It became obvious to me they only gave their attention to the things that *qualified* for it. They had uncluttered their life of anything not related to their Assignment and calling. *They had tasted failure, therefore they did not fear it.*

Some years ago, I read where the wife of a world famous evangelist was asked a question.

"How does it feel to have your husband gone for long lengths of time away from you and the children? What is your opinion of him being home for just a few days each year?"

She replied from a deep reservoir of Wisdom, *"I would rather have a slice of a great man than the whole of an average man."*

Any woman who pursues greatness is worth pursuing.

My own mother is a monument in my memory of such appetites. We were poor, but she never stopped reading and collecting books for us children. I still never get enough books for my library to this very day. She awakened my thirst for information and knowledge. She knew that a *single success secret* in a book was worth the price of the entire book.

Celebrate any woman whose bookshelves are as crammed as her clothes closet. Celebrate the woman who sits in seminars, goes to the local library, browses through the book store and *would rather have a book than a manicure.* (Nothing is wrong with investing in your personal appearance. It is important. But, *greatness also requires investment.*)

It is an *Unforgettable Woman* who takes the time to invest in the accumulation of knowledge and Wisdom.

All extraordinary people are not necessarily enjoyable people. Some geniuses in life who contain rare gifts are sometimes obnoxious, embittered and cynical. It is the unforgettable and extraordinary protégé who refuses to be deterred from pursuing and insists on extracting the gold within an extraordinary person.

That's what will make *you*, too, *unforgettable.*

≈ 11 ≈

THE UNFORGETTABLE WOMAN MAKES WISE DECISIONS

She married the man—who had a godly mother.

She was loyal to the *right person*—who lived a godly life.

She worked in the *right fields*—where great men could observe and assess her productivity.

One of the greatest decisions you will ever make in your lifetime is the marriage decision. When you marry someone, you are forever connected and welded to their *weaknesses* as well as to their strengths.

Consider well the mentors of your mate. What did his father teach him? What did his mother teach him? What philosophy has been branded into his conscience?

Ruth married the son of a godly woman. So she was forever linked to spiritual Wisdom, a spiritual well that would supply her like an oasis in the middle of her emotional deserts.

When you are dating someone, ask yourself *important* questions. Honest questions. *Revealing* questions. Who is their spiritual oasis in their time of emptiness? To whom do they go when there is great temptation in their personal life? Who advises them when crisis occurs?

Your mentors reveal much about your future.

Ruth made wise decisions in her loyalties. It is not enough to simply be loyal to a person. *Displaced loyalty is a frequent tragedy.*

What is displaced loyalty? It is when you are loyal to someone who is not genuine, real and of God. Ruth was loyal, and that is admirable. But she was loyal to a woman with character, integrity and great Wisdom. That's what made her unforgettable.

Thoroughly review your loyalty—to each person in your life. Displaced loyalty is tragic, unfortunate and produces devastating results. Many in organized crime are loyal to each other. They cover and excuse many criminal acts. *Displaced loyalty justifies wrong actions of those we love.* We cover for them. We lie for them. We shield them.

Never bond with a rebel. "And have no fellowship with the unfruitful works of darkness, but rather reprove them," (Ephesians 5:11).

Do not make peace with an angry man. Do not get bonded to someone when they are in a position against authority.

When you bond with a rebel, you are forever welded to the future disasters he has scheduled.

Look at the Israelites. Those who sided with Achan were stoned. Those who sided with Korah were destroyed.

Ruth had enough Wisdom to focus her loyalty and make a commitment to someone who had character—Naomi, who had *earned* her loyalty.

She worked among those who honored greatness.

I believe geography matters in your personal success. Your *place of Assignment* is vital to your joy.

You see, it is possible to invest your entire life and pour yourself out for someone who does not recognize greatness, faithfulness and loyalty.

Joseph worked for an ungodly man, Potiphar. But Potiphar recognized greatness when he saw it and promoted it. Pharaoh was not necessarily a wonderful, godly example. But he knew greatness and extraordinary gifts when he saw them. He promoted Joseph.

If you have been working on your job for 20 years and have never seen significant changes, think again. *Refuse to work for a boss that does not recognize the gifts of God within you.* Make a wise decision.

Most successful companies have this quality. Companies that never grow lack this quality.

You must have Wisdom to make changes.

Any Movement Toward Order Creates Pleasure.

-MIKE MURDOCK

≈ 12 ≈

THE UNFORGETTABLE WOMAN MAKES DECISIONS THAT ALWAYS MOVE HER LIFE IN THE RIGHT DIRECTION

When she married her husband, she married into a godly family. I am certain their marriage had its ups and downs. There were times of great anger, turmoil and confusion which happen in many marriages. Undoubtedly, there were nights of anguish and tears of doubt.

But, her decision was made in the *right direction*— a godly, upright and spiritually-conscious family.

This is the criteria for good decision-making. This is how to monitor your personal ability to make wise decisions: *Is it taking my life in the right direction?*

As one girl said to me, "I broke up with my boyfriend."

"Why?" I asked.

"He refuses to serve the Lord whole-heartedly."

"How do you feel about that decision?" I queried.

"Well, I get very lonely at times. There are no Christian boys in my church that I have a true interest in," she replied. "But somehow I know The Holy Spirit is pleased with my decision. God will eventually reward me for it. *At least, I know I am going in the right direction with my life."*

There is a gold mine of Wisdom in this, believe me.

I spoke to a young man who was a great musician in a night club in Las Vegas. He had decided to quit the band. He replied that though it was something he'd done his entire life, "I must move in the *right direction* with my life. As long as I am entertaining others in an atmosphere of alcoholism, drunkenness and lust, God cannot prosper me."

He was learning the secret of making decisions that *move your life in the right direction.*

Let me illustrate: Suppose you see a beautiful car that excites you. You don't have the money for it. Your present car is 4 years old. You would have to borrow the entire cost, but you have really taken to heart the teachings of Deuteronomy 28:12, "The Lord shall open unto thee His good treasure, the Heavens to give the rain unto thy land in His season, and to bless all the work of thine hand: and *thou shalt lend unto many nations, and thou shalt not borrow."*

You refuse to borrow the money. You insist on driving your same car for another year—*until* the Lord provides the full amount for the car.

Some would call you crazy. Some would think you are being overly sensitive and misinterpreting the Scriptures. In fact, some would show you on paper how you could get everything that you are wanting—except you would be moving your entire life and family *toward debt.* "The rich ruleth over the poor, and the borrower is servant to the lender," (Proverbs 22:7).

When you refuse that car loan, you are *moving your life in the right direction*—toward being debt-free.

Suppose you are called into the ministry? You may

already have a scholarship to a secular college. Someone
may have already offered to pay your way to a major law
university. But in your heart, you know you are
supposed to sit under spiritual mentors, studying
spiritual laws instead of earthly laws. So you move to a
city to attend a Bible college. You go to Bible college 4
hours a day and work the other 8 hours a day to put
yourself through Bible school.

Why is this wise? You are making decisions that
move your life in the right direction.

Are you overweight? Certainly you will find friends
that tell you, "I love you exactly the way you are. In fact,
I can't even picture you being skinny!"

But there is a cry in the depth of you for good health
and to walk in excellence in every part of your life. You
start attending seminars about weight loss and physical
fitness. You begin to walk 5 minutes every morning to
start moving your body—you're wise. Why? *You are
making decisions that move your life in the right
direction.*

You can become unforgettable to everyone you meet.

Persistence Is Not
A Chosen Virtue...
But Rather
The Product of
An Obsession.

-MIKE MURDOCK

≈ 13 ≈

THE UNFORGETTABLE WOMAN IS PERSISTENT

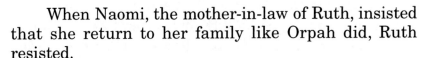

When Naomi, the mother-in-law of Ruth, insisted that she return to her family like Orpah did, Ruth resisted.

She had a *goal.*

She had a *photograph* of her future.

She *knew* exactly what she wanted.

She persisted.

What is persistence? It means to go on stubbornly in spite of difficulties. It means to continue despite opposition.

How do you birth persistence? I believe that persistence is a quality produced within you...when *you become consumed with a desired end result for your life.* Your major concern is *not how* to get it...nor *when* to get it...nor *how many* friends share your desire. Rather, *persistence is produced by an obsession with a desired conclusion.*

Jesus put it this way, "And ye shall be hated of all men for My name's sake: but he that endureth to the end shall be saved," (Matthew 10:22).

"And Jesus said unto him, No man, having put his hand to the plough, and looking back, is fit for the kingdom of God," (Luke 9:62).

Do you remember Job? James wrote, "Behold, we

count them happy which endure. Ye have heard of the patience of Job, and have seen the end of the Lord; that the Lord is very pitiful, and of tender mercy," (James 5:11). What does this mean? Those who are persistent have tasted inside the depth of their hearts what their desired miracle and conclusion is going to be.

Everybody would like to be persistent in the pursuit of their dreams and goals. Most do not *remain* persistent. Why?

They simply do not yet possess a thorough and persuasive photograph of their desired future. Doubts exist. There is lack of focus. They are not *yet* consumed with it.

Their *minds* are *divided.*

Their *hearts* are *divided.*

Their *focus* is *divided.* They have not yet abandoned themselves to their desired goal. They have not completely abandoned their present situation. *They are divided between two worlds.*

David cried, "My heart is fixed, O God, my heart is fixed: I will sing and give praise," (Psalm 57:7).

Paul insisted, "Brethren, I count not myself to have apprehended: but this one thing I do, forgetting those things which are behind, and reaching forth unto those things which are before," (Philippians 3:13).

Joshua instructed, "Only be thou strong and very courageous, that thou mayest observe to do according to all the law, which Moses My servant commanded thee: turn not from it to the right hand or to the left, that thou mayest prosper whithersoever thou goest. This book of the law shall not depart out of thy mouth; but thou shalt meditate therein day and night, that thou mayest observe to do according to all that is written therein: for then thou shalt make thy way prosperous, and then thou shalt have good success," (Joshua 1:7-8).

Elijah asked, "How long halt ye between two opinions? if the Lord be God, follow Him: but if Baal, then follow him. And the people answered him not a word," (1 Kings 18:21).

Joshua said, "And if it seem evil unto you to serve the Lord, choose you this day whom ye will serve; whether the gods which your fathers served that were on the other side of the flood, or the gods of the Amorites, in whose land ye dwell: but as for me and my house, we will serve the Lord," (Joshua 24:15).

Paul said, "Ye did run well; who did hinder you that ye should not obey the truth," (Galatians 5:7).

Persistence requires total focus.

Focus requires ruthlessness in dealing with distractions in your life.

Make sure that what you are pursuing is truly ordered of the Lord.

Have quality mentors supervising your life and confirming those things God has spoken to your heart.

Walk holy and pure before God so that your motives and heart remain right before Him.

Depend entirely upon The Holy Spirit to impart the endurance you need.

There Are Two Ways
       To Increase Wisdom:
Mistakes And Mentors.

-*MIKE MURDOCK*

≈ 14 ≈

THE UNFORGETTABLE WOMAN RESPECTS THE MENTORSHIP OF AN OLDER AND MORE EXPERIENCED WOMAN

Ruth had not remarried when she followed Naomi back to Bethlehem.

She worked hard. One day, Naomi expressed that it was time for her to have a husband in her life. She advised her to go to the threshing floor where Boaz worked every night. Naomi knew the habits of extraordinary men.

Great men simply have great habits.

She advised Ruth to avoid discussions with him while he was having supper or even working. She instructed Ruth that there would be an *appropriate time* that Boaz would awaken, see her and discuss any details regarding a relationship.

Ruth *listened.* She followed the instructions. And history records the incredible parade of benefits that followed.

Ruth was *teachable.* Boaz had instructed her to restrict her work and the gathering of food to his fields alone and to not go into other fields. Naomi had given the same instructions. Ruth followed them.

Hearing good advice is *not* the key to success.

Applying good advice is the key to extraordinary success.

One of my pastor friends has had remarkable success in his ministry. He shared with me one day an important key concerning counseling.

"Mike, I refuse to counsel anyone personally until they have sat in every single service in which I have ministered for a period of 6 weeks. If their questions and problems have not been resolved through my teaching over a 6-week period, I will schedule a personal counseling session with them. In that session, I give specific instructions to be followed. If they do not follow those instructions, I refuse to give a second counseling session. It is a waste of my time and theirs, if they refuse to implement the Wisdom I impart."

You can predict the success of someone by their ability to follow an instruction.

I am praying that God returns a real respect for the elderly of our generation. Some older women in our generation have more insight and Wisdom in their little finger than many young girls will have within the next 20 years of their lives.

Elisha sat at the feet of Elijah.

Timothy sat at the feet of Paul.

Esther listened to Mordecai and the eunuch who advised her.

Joshua sat at the feet of Moses.

Your mentor foresees problems you cannot see coming.

Are you planning to enter the field of real estate?

Find the most successful and productive realtor within 100 miles. Establish a friendship. Become the protégé.

Do you long for a useful ministry? Find a man or woman of God to serve. Carry their briefcase. Shine their shoes. Baby-sit their children. Clean their house. Wash their car. *Do whatever is necessary to access their anointing, connect with their climate and attach yourself to their atmosphere.*

Whatever is growing in them will begin to grow within you. Whatever they have decided to starve will die within you.

Ruth applied good advice when she heard it. It made her *unforgettable.*

What You Make Happen
For Others,
God Will Make Happen
For You.

-MIKE MURDOCK

∾ 15 ∾

THE UNFORGETTABLE WOMAN TREATS HER MOTHER-IN-LAW BETTER THAN 7 SONS WOULD TREAT THEIR MOTHER

The women of the city said this to Naomi, "...for thy daughter in law, which loveth thee, which is better to thee than seven sons," (Ruth 4:15).

It is a rare woman who treats other women kindly.

It's quite interesting sometimes to watch a lady approach a couple. It is sad to watch some women respond in a flattering way to the husband and almost ignore his wife completely. Yet it happens every day.

Ruth established a reputation for taking care of her mother-in-law. Boaz explained to Ruth why he had taken the time to invest favor, attention and provision into her life. "And Boaz answered and said unto her, It hath fully been shewed me, all that thou hast done unto thy mother in law since the death of thine husband," (Ruth 2:11).

This explains favor.

It explains good fortune.

It explains miracles.

It explains why good things happen to people.

In Proverbs 31:26, the Bible explains *The Unforgettable Woman:* "...and in her tongue is the law of kindness."

When you see someone mistreat another, you know immediately that in due time you will be on the receiving end of that anger. *Never trust anyone who treats another person unkindly.* What they do to them, they will eventually do to you.

Some years ago I dated a young lady who spoke rather harshly to her mother. The Holy Spirit revealed to me quite accurately that her reaction to authority revealed deep problems within her that would later emerge in any marriage. Some days later, I heard her lie to her mother on the telephone. I recognized instantly that it was only a matter of time until she would be lying to me as well. The relationship ended. As far as I know, she has continued in these problems for many years.

Ruth is extraordinary. Unforgettable. She knows *her treatment of others determines how God will treat her.*

I have made Ephesians 6:8 a personal motto: *What You Make Happen For Others, God Will Make Happen For You.*

As tears of joy and appreciation filled my eyes one day, I looked across my home at what God had given me and asked the Lord a question: "Why have You been so good to me?" Instantly, The Holy Spirit spoke back to my heart, "Because you have *honored* your mother and father."

I really believe *your treatment of your parents affects you for your lifetime.* "Honor thy father and mother; which is the first commandment with promise; That it may be well with thee, and thou mayest live long on the earth," (Ephesians 6:2-3).

Americans lack this respect in a very tragic sense. I have spent a lot of time in East Africa and noted with great joy how children there respect their elders in their tribes in a marvelous way. They reverence them. They listen to them. They even permit them to eat first. I was in a little village several years ago where the children sat outside the hut waiting for me to finish eating with the chieftain and his wives. They would not dare barge in or interrupt.

We need to return to respecting those who rule, those in authority over us. It will unleash a wave of blessing beyond anything ever imagined.

Ruth respected authority. It made her *unforgettable*.

Someone Is Always
Observing You Who Is
Capable of Greatly
Blessing You.

-MIKE MURDOCK

❧ 16 ❧

The Unforgettable Woman Is Honest And Open About Her Needs And Her Poverty

Ruth was a widow.

She was taking care of her mother-in-law, Naomi, who was widowed.

She was a foreigner.

She had no husband to provide for her.

She had no children to provide for her.

She had no parents to provide for her.

She was impoverished and broke.

Yet she had integrity, honesty and remarkable candor and openness about her needs. She approached the servants and said, "I pray you, let me glean and gather after the reapers among the sheaves." *She asked permission to get the leftovers.*

God had instructed those who were blessed of Israel, "And when ye reap the Harvest of your land, thou shalt not wholly reap the corners of thy field, neither shalt thou gather the gleanings of thy Harvest. And thou shalt not glean thy vineyard, neither shalt thou gather every grape of thy vineyard; thou shalt leave them for the poor and stranger: I am the Lord your God," (Leviticus 19:9-10).

Ruth was both poor and a stranger. She made no attempt to hide it. *She did not try to act like someone she was not.* She was open about her needs.

Some people are going broke these days trying to appear rich.

We even buy fake diamond rings to make others think we are really prosperous.

Dignity is admirable.

Elegance is desirable.

Yet there is something very precious about someone humble enough to be vulnerable to others. Ruth had this kind of humility.

I know there are exceptions. Let me be very frank with you. I realize that we are barraged at times with *professional* beggars, those who want handouts and think the world owes them a living. I admit it gets wearisome to see the same faces and the same people who stay in trouble week after week after week, over a period of years. They do not solve problems for others, consequently, they may never have any money. They refuse to ask for a job when they have discovered that asking for a handout is easier.

Some very precious people, consequently, have *refused to share the intimate pain they are experiencing.* As a result, none of us are able to reach out and participate in their recovery.

This is why, for several years now, I have been trying to get pastors to establish a "Seed-Faith Team" in their local churches. Suppose the church members include a plumber, a realtor, a mechanic, a roofer and a lawyer. When one of the *widows* of the local church has her car break down, she can call the Seed-Faith Team at her local church. The mechanic on the Seed-Faith Team will joyfully go and repair her automobile...as a Seed...just to bless to her. When her roof leaks, she can call the Seed-Faith Team at the church. The roofer, a member of the Seed-Faith Team, can go and repair her roof in his free time as a gift to her, a Seed for the Lord.

Two things are needed here: 1) You must be honest about your own needs to those in authority over you, and 2) Look for those who are troubled, frustrated and devastated by losses.

▶ *Someone In Trouble Is Always Your Door Out of Trouble.*

▶ *Your Vulnerability Will Always Link You To A Champion.*

▶ *Lack Is Always Your Link To A Provider.*

Face it. Confess it. Enjoy a miracle. One of the sad and unfortunate attitudes that prosperity teaching has birthed is this obsession with being first class, excellent and elitist. I have known of ministers of the Gospel who were infuriated when they received an airline ticket in coach, proclaiming, "I will only fly in the first-class cabin—I am a child of the King." Meanwhile, they sit in the seat preparing their sermon on Jesus who was born in a manger and went to a cross so that we might have eternal life.

I believe in excellence.

I believe in doing things in the highest quality way.

But an attitude of humility is really the highest level God wants us to know and experience.

It makes you *unforgettable.*

Your Rewards In Life
Are Determined By
The Kinds of Problems You
Are Willing To Solve
For Others.

MIKE MURDOCK

⋙ 17 ⋘

THE UNFORGETTABLE WOMAN IS SERIOUS ABOUT HER WORK

————⟫●⟪————

Ruth *asked* for permission to labor in the fields of Boaz.

She wanted to work.

There is no record that she applied to the local welfare department to feed herself and her widowed mother-in-law. She has not complained. She has not whined and griped over bad treatment. She is not sobbing at the altar of the local church about her husband leaving her no insurance money when he died.

She loves work.

She has *searched* out a place to work.

She has *asked* permission to work.

There is no indication that anyone has pushed and begged her to "get a job." Naomi did not kick her out of bed every morning. She has not sought out a husband so she can "stay at home for a change."

This woman is quite serious about *being productive* with her life.

She wants to *make a difference.*

She is quite serious *about earning her way through life.*

Her work style attracted the attention of the reapers

and the servants of Boaz. When Boaz asked his supervisor about Ruth, he said, "And she said, I pray you, let me glean and gather after the reapers among the sheaves: so she came, and hath continued even from the morning until now, that she tarried a little in the house," (Ruth 2:7).

She did not ask for extra barley to be given her. She did not say, "I am really poor, could you have Boaz give a donation to me and my widowed mother-in-law?"

She had not even approached Boaz, the wealthy landowner, for a donation!

She was *serious* about work.

She was so serious about it, that the supervisor had noticed that she had not even stopped except for a few minutes in the shade, but had worked diligently from morning to night.

Your boss may be out of town this week. But those who work around you know whether you simply create flurry and movement, or whether you are truly productive in your job. Let me say again, your boss probably won't ask you about your productivity. Instead, he will consult with those who are supervisors, *his trusted employees who study your activity.*

It is my personal opinion that truly great employees are really rare. It seems that so many want to receive good salaries for average productivity. I have even known of some who sit at the time clock 15 and 20 minutes ahead of time, anxious to leave their work and get home. If you are coming in late every day and wanting to leave early...rethink your job position. You are working on the wrong job, or else you have developed a bad attitude toward your job.

The work place should be a happy place for you.

It should be a place of *significance,* great joy and a

sense of productivity in your life.

Here Are 8 Evidences That You Are A Serious Achiever

1.   You Have A Written Plan For The Day. Your planner contains specific *tasks* connected to specific *times* for their achievement. It contains a follow-up sheet of people and projects to follow up on.

2.   You Write Down Instructions. You *repeat them* back to your boss, so there are no misunderstandings. You do it.

3.   You Consult With Your Boss Regularly. You seek any areas of improvement or correction he might suggest.

4.   You Search For Seminars To Attend. You want to be equipped for your job and qualified to be the best you can be.

5.   You Dress Appropriately And With Dignity. You want to represent your company well if the boss should bring special guests in through the offices.

6.   You Are Swift To Accept Extra Responsibility. You don't mind if in a crisis, or to complete a necessary project, overtime is necessary.

7.   You Motivate Others Around You. You encourage others around you to return to their jobs, instead of fudging on lunch time.

8.   You Look For Solutions To Problems Around You.

It is what makes an *Unforgettable Woman.*

You Will Only
Be Remembered In Life
For Two Things:
The Problems You Solve
or The Ones You Create.

-MIKE MURDOCK

≈ 18 ≈

The Unforgettable Woman Finds That Productive Men Are Responsive To Productive Women

When the supervisor informed Boaz that the damsel working was Ruth, and that she was the daughter-in-law of Naomi, he also informed him that she had requested permission to work and glean in the fields. He told Boaz she was very productive and had only taken a few minutes off work the entire day.

Boaz then took the initiative to approach Ruth. He instructed her to feel free to glean in his field only, and not feel a need to go elsewhere. *He wanted to be involved in her life.*

Productivity is magnetic.

When Jesus called disciples, they were all busy, *doing* something. Some were fishing. Some were collecting taxes. Even Saul (before he became the Apostle Paul) was very diligent in putting Christians in prison, when God spoke to him on the Damascus Road and called him into the service of the ministry.

You are commanded to *multiply.*

God *reacts* to productivity, also.

Notice these examples: When the man with one talent refused to use his talent, he was cast into outer darkness, and what he had was taken away from him. (See Matthew 25:14-30.)

"And seeing a fig tree afar off having leaves, He came, if haply He might find anything thereon: and when He came to it, He found nothing but leaves; for the time of figs was not yet. And Jesus answered and said unto it, No man eat fruit of thee hereafter for ever. And His disciples heard it," (Mark 11:13-14).

It appears that God *kills anything that refuses to increase and multiply.*

You see, the very first instruction God gave everything He made was to *multiply* and *increase.* Birds, animals and people. Even plants and trees are commanded to become more, increase and multiply. "And God blessed them, saying, Be fruitful, and multiply, and fill the waters in the seas, and let fowl multiply in the earth," (Genesis 1:22).

It is unnatural to *decrease.*

It is natural to *increase.*

When you do the right things, you will attract the right people into your life.

When you do the wrong things, you will attract the wrong people into your life.

When you walk in obedience, you attract people who are comfortable with obedience.

When you walk in disobedience, you attract people who are comfortable with disobedience.

When you are lazy, you will attract lazy people in your life.

When you are diligent, you will attract diligent people into your life.

This is one of the glorious rewards of doing the right thing, being productive and multiplying yourself. You see, everything right begins to come into your life because you are the *current* that attracts.

You do not have to be a businesswoman with your own organization to be productive. You can be productive right there in your home every day. You can be productive in the activities of your church, in the rebuilding of a healthy body or in the pursuit of education at your local college.

Never underestimate the incredible, unavoidable currents and benefits of *productivity* in your life.

It is one of the great secrets of becoming the *Unforgettable Woman.*

You Are Never As Far From A Miracle As It First Appears.

-MIKE MURDOCK

≈ 19 ≈

THE UNFORGETTABLE WOMAN DISCOVERS SOMEONE IS ALWAYS OBSERVING YOU WHO IS CAPABLE OF GREATLY BLESSING YOU

Successful people are *observant* people.

They notice their *surroundings.*

They study human *behavior.*

They notice human *reactions.*

Any employer notes laziness instantly. Any boss can tell you who the slow movers are on his staff as well as those who move quickly. It does not necessarily mean that they react instantly to it. Lazy people are not always fired immediately. Diligent people are not always promoted immediately.

Patterns are studied.

Attitudes are noted.

Promotions are *eventual.*

Boaz, the wealthy landowner, discusses Ruth with his workers one day.

"Who's damsel is this?"

"It is the Moabitish damsel that came back with Naomi out of the country of Moab: And she said, I pray you, let me glean and gather after the reapers among the sheaves: so she came, and hath continued even from the morning until now, that she tarried a little in the house," (Ruth 2:5-7).

Employees notice the most diligent among themselves also. Employees talk to bosses, too.

Bosses listen to trusted employees. It is quite often that the words of the most trusted employees determine the promotion and salary raises that bosses give throughout the company.

Likewise, it is often the words of a trusted employee that *prevent* someone from getting a raise or a promotion.

That is why it is so foolish to be lazy on your job. Those around you have to carry your part of the workload. They eventually resent you for it. *Their resentment is often spoken into the ears of the only one who can promote you.*

Attitudes become known in the same manner. When one employee is disgruntled or embittered, it permeates and poisons the atmosphere. Eventually, a trusted employee will report it to the supervisor. His removal then is guaranteed. "Know ye not that a little leaven leaveneth the whole lump?" (1 Corinthians 5:6).

"Be not deceived: evil communications corrupt good manners," (1 Corinthians 15:33).

"Where no wood is, there the fire goeth out: so where there is no talebearer, the strife ceaseth," (Proverbs 26:20).

Never forget this. *Your attitude, conduct and behavior is continually being reported to somebody...somewhere...sometime.*

"Therefore whatsoever ye have spoken in darkness shall be heard in the light; and that which ye have spoken in the ear in closets shall be proclaimed upon the housetops," (Luke 12:3). Obviously, critics observe you. They constantly study your flaws, discuss them and gossip. Ignore the great temptation to become responsive to critics. Suddenly, their opinion can become your focus. You will strive to justify your behavior or become entangled in an internal campaign to prove them wrong.

Don't fall for it.

Critics rarely present a plan for improvement. They are not builders. They are destroyers.

Never build your life around the opinion of a critic.

Rather, become conscious that whoever God has ordained to be your golden connection to the next season of your life—*is presently observing you.*

They study your reactions in a crisis.

They note your response to criticism and correction.

They listen for an attitude of humility, kindness and graciousness.

Your acts of mercy are documented.

Every Good Quality In You Is Obvious And Noticeable To The One God Has Called To Promote You.

Ruth did not have to "sell" herself to Boaz. She did not have to speak persuasively and coyly nor be flirtatious with his servants.

In fact, let me reassure you that had she been flirting with the workers, Boaz would have been the first person to know it. News travels. People discuss each other.

And consequently, Ruth would never have become Mrs. Boaz.

Great People Notice Great Qualities.

So don't become discouraged when criticism hits you from every side.

Don't become frustrated when it seems that promotion is coming slowly, and you wonder if God really has noticed your hard efforts and consistency to please Him.

There is a Boaz scheduled in your future.

He may already be in your present season.

There is a strong possibility that he already knows you by name and is making plans to bless you and cause great experiences in your life.

Somebody is saying some good things about you today.

Somebody sees the rare qualities within you.

Something incredible is being spoken about your life.

Somebody is planning to reward you.

They are closer than you even realize.

Your faith will decide when it happens.

Your *attitude* schedules it.

So keep your focus on *obedience.*

Keep your focus on doing *the right things.*

When you keep doing the right things, the right people will enter your life.

When you keep doing the right things, *the wrong people will disconnect from you.*

When you keep doing the right things, news gets around.

When you keep doing the right things, *promotion is guaranteed.*

"Boaz went over and talked to her, Listen, my child, he said to her. Stay right here with us to glean; don't think of going to any other fields. Stay right behind my women workers; I have warned the young men not to bother you; when you are thirsty, go and help yourself to the water," (Ruth 2:8-9 LB). Boaz told his young men to let her glean right among the sheaves without stopping her, and to snap off some heads of barley and drop them on purpose for her to glean, and not to make any remarks. (See verses 15 and 16.)

Never forget this.

Your father is noting your response to his correction. Your mother senses your desire to show mercy to your sisters and brothers.

Your brothers and sisters eventually get a report on your true attitude and feelings about them.

Your boss discovers quicker than you could possibly realize when you disagree with an instruction he has given you.

Somebody is observing you today who is in position to launch the greatest season of miracles you have ever known in your entire lifetime.

Don't take it lightly. Guard your words. Guard your attitude.

"A good name is rather to be chosen than great riches," (Proverbs 22:1).

It will make you *unforgettable.*

When God Wants To Bless You, He Brings A Person Into Your Life.

-MIKE MURDOCK

≈ 20 ≈

THE UNFORGETTABLE WOMAN DISCOVERS GOD CAN GET ANYONE TO YOU ANYWHERE YOU ARE

Ruth was an impoverished Moabite peasant girl in the fields.

Yet 24 hours later, the man of her dreams was connected to her life.

It can happen in a single day.

It can happen within 24 hours.

Miracles happen as quickly as tragedies.

God is a geographical genius.

He is Master of the real estate He owns.

It is true that He owns the cattle on a thousand hills. It is also true that He knows *where* every hill is—and *where* every cow is located.

Peter was instructed to go fishing...because Jesus knew exactly where the fish was located that contained the money for their taxes.

God saw the widow of Zarephath starving...and within 24 hours had connected her to Elijah who radically and dramatically changed her lifestyle.

David was tending sheep. He was alone. He was playing his harp and soothing the sheep. He seemed to be a long distance from where the action was taking place. His brothers were known soldiers under Saul. He was just a shepherd boy.

Within 24 hours, his name was a household word in Israel. God had connected him to Goliath and the greatest victory of his life.

God sees you. "Are not five sparrows sold for two farthings, and not one of them is forgotten before God? But even the very hairs of your head are all numbered. Fear not therefore: ye are of more value than many sparrows," (Luke 12:6-7).

God wants to give to you. "Every good gift and every perfect gift is from above, and cometh down from the Father of lights, with Whom is no variableness, neither shadow of turning," (James 1:17).

God wants you to have good things. "No good thing will He withhold from them that walk uprightly," (Psalm 84:11).

When God Gets Ready To Bless You, He Puts A Person In Your Life.

Do you feel like David today, stuck out on the hillside tending the sheep while the action is taking place in another part of the world? *God can send for you within 24 hours.*

Do you sometimes feel like Moses, stuck on the backside of a desert, taking care of the flocks for a father-in-law? Within 24 hours, you may be standing in the court of the leaders of your day.

Do you feel like the starving widow, stuck with the responsibilities of a child, and you don't know where your next meal is going to come from? Focus your faith.

An Elijah is receiving an instruction to walk into your life and unleash the flow of your faith. *Your famine is over.*

Do you feel like the lame man at the gate Beautiful? Do you feel that everyone else gets the attention and the opportunities for miracles but you?

Something is about to happen. God is scheduling a divine connection for you...today.

Somebody has spoken your name this morning...that you have not even met.

*Someone has discussed you this week...*that God is sending into your life.

You have asked the Lord for a specific miracle...a specific person to come into your life and turn the currents.

You are not out of range.

You have *not* been *forgotten* by God.

Your circumstances are perfect for a miracle.

Joseph could easily have said, "I am in prison. How in the world will I ever reach the palace with this stain on my reputation?" Twenty-four hours later he was the prime minister.

God Can Get You Anywhere He Wants You To Be...Within 24 Hours.

The Unforgettable Woman knows this.

The Quickest Cure For Ingratitude Is Loss.

-MIKE MURDOCK

≈ 21 ≈

The Unforgettable Woman Is Thankful And Appreciative

Ruth was *appreciative.*

Appreciative means showing appreciation of someone or something: to be grateful.

It is interesting to note the reaction of Ruth when Boaz gave her permission to stay in his field and glean barley. She thanked him warmly. "How can you be so kind to me?" she asked. "You must know I am only a foreigner," (Ruth 2:10-11 LB).

She continues on in verse 13, "Oh, thank you, sir," she replied. "You are so good to me, and I'm not even one of your workers!" She did not *assume* that it was *owed* her. She really did not even ask for extra favor. She valued the smallest crumb or barley left in her behalf.

Appreciative people have a magnetism to them. Their ability to value acts of kindness inspire us and make us want to perform accordingly.

Jessica is a beautiful little 9-year-old girl in Minneapolis, Minnesota. She is so articulate, expressive and appreciative. Every time I have done something special for her, she looks up with those big beautiful eyes and the biggest smile you can imagine, and says, "Oh, thank you so very much!" It is that attitude of appreciation that makes children so delightful and makes us want to produce for them.

It is often said that Christmas is for children. Now why do we say this when it is celebrated as the birthday of Jesus of Nazareth? Why doesn't every one of us enjoy Christmas like children?

Children *appreciate.*

They celebrate gifts.

Gifts are great events to them.

It is so unfortunate that after some of us receive so many gifts and blessings for so many years our ability to appreciate seems to deteriorate and diminish dramatically. Work on this in your personal life. Work on this in your home. Do not take for granted that your husband is "supposed to bring home the paycheck." Don't assume that it's "a woman's place to clean up the house and prepare the meals."

Appreciation of those around you will make you unforgettable.

Find ways to express your appreciation.

Do it *verbally.* Speak kind words of appreciation.

Do it *privately.* When no one else is around, be gentle in expressing your true appreciation and gratefulness.

Do it *publicly.* Others need to hear that you know and appreciate what God has blessed you with.

Do it *often.* Not just once a year at a birthday or an anniversary.

Do it *generously.* Go the extra mile when you buy a gift for someone special whom you love and appreciate.

Do it *thoughtfully.* One of my closest friends in Sarasota, Florida, sent me two books a few weeks ago. What kind of books? The very author that he knows I love to read. He had put *thought* into the purchase of my gifts. He knew what I wanted to read. I've had many people give me books *they* thought I *ought* to read...very few have purchased me books that I *wanted* to read.

Do it *quickly.* If someone has blessed your life significantly, do not wait several months or years to express it. Try to establish the habit of responding to an act of kindness *within 72 hours.*

Do it *cheerfully.* When you express your appreciation, do not do it grudgingly as if it is a pain or an effort.

You will become *unforgettable* to every friend in your life.

The Worth of Any
Relationship Can Be
Measured By Its Influence
On Your Priorities.

-MIKE MURDOCK

≈ 22 ≈

The Unforgettable Woman Is Knowledgeable of The Business of The Man In Her Life

Ruth *worked* in the fields of Boaz. She worked among his employees and staff.

She *heard* their conversations.

They knew her.

There was constant exchange, day after day. Obviously, when Boaz wanted to discuss his business, she was already comfortable with the conversation. She knew the needs of his workers. I'm sure she would see equipment break down and know about it. She was aware, alert and informed.

In the underground world, I am told that many in organized crime never discuss anything with their wives. Their wives simply keep the house and children. They are kept ignorant of the activities of their husbands.

Ignorance is dangerous.

It is deadly.

It robs you of the strongest bond with your man—*his passion for his work.*

It is one of the biggest reasons marriages fail.

You can never understand your man by studying him.

You must study what he studies.

You must *look* at the same things he gazes upon *daily.*

You must *learn* to discuss what he loves to discuss.

You must learn to *think* the thoughts he *longs to think.*

You must be comfortable to go the *same direction* he is going.

Few women really grasp the flow of their husband's passion, his work.

This explains why many illicit affairs begin on the job. One unfortunate minister told me weeping, "My ministry was destroyed because of my relationship with my secretary. Mike, she was not more attractive than my wife. She was not even more sensuous. *She simply understood the problems I was trying to solve every day.* She was there when I needed to vent and express myself. She became a sounding board to me."

I plead with wives everywhere: *Become knowledgeable of the problems your husband has dedicated himself to solve with his life.*

The secret of a man is in his memories.

Encourage the expression of his thoughts.

Understand his memories.

Permit his spoken fears without giving advice.

Permit him to speak without interruptions of trivia.

Give total attention when he speaks.

Listen *thoroughly.*

Ask thoughtful questions.

It is my personal opinion that the most enjoyable

women in the world are those who ask you the greatest questions. So give your mate a chance to discuss his passion and obsession.

"Don't bring your work home!" is the cry of marriage manuals.

How ridiculous! *Any person who is succeeding with his life brings his work with him wherever he goes.* It consumes his mind. It is his life passion. He loves to discuss it continually.

(Exceptions occur, of course, especially when everyone at your house is not truly interested or informed. Any conversation often becomes burdensome with such people.)

However, it is a Master Secret of *The Unforgettable Woman.*

The Seasons of Your Life
Will Change
Every Time You Use
Your Faith.

-MIKE MURDOCK

≈ 23 ≈

The Unforgettable Woman Knows When The Seasons of Her Life Are Changing

———————➤➋●◄———————

Ruth had tasted the joys of intimacy and the disappointments of normal marriage. She was raised in the comfort of her home country. Yet when her greatest source of mentorship chose to make a change, she *cooperated.*

God never changes.

But, *the seasons do change.*

Moses experienced his season in the palace of Egypt. But when he became a deliverer, *his heart began to change* as he observed the slavery of his brethren. His seasons had changed, and he discerned it.

Elijah was sent to the brook. The ravens fed him. But one day the brook dried up and the ravens did not show up. *Lack was a signal. The season of change had arrived.* It was time to make traveling plans down to Zarephath.

Carefully note your present circumstances. Is it possible that you have exhausted the benefits of your present season? Could God possibly be giving you pieces of a new puzzle to put together? Do you find thoughts consuming you of another place and another season, instead of focusing on your present?

Be good to yourself. Take note when God schedules a transition in your life. It might not happen suddenly. It might be a slow changing, but change is absolutely guaranteed when God works His schedule of *promotion.*

"Remember ye not the former things, neither consider the things of old. Behold, I will do a new thing; now it shall spring forth; shall ye not know it? I will even make a way in the wilderness, and rivers in the desert," (Isaiah 43:18-19).

Sing New Songs. "Sing unto Him a new song; play skilfully with a loud noise," (Psalm 33:3).

"And He hath put a new song in my mouth," (Psalm 40:3).

Ask For The New Wine. "So shall thy barns be filled with plenty, and thy presses shall burst out with new wine," (Proverbs 3:10).

Be Thankful For Your New Name. Isaiah 62:2 says, "And the Gentiles shall see thy righteousness, and all kings thy glory: and thou shalt be called by a new name, which the mouth of the Lord shall name."

Receive A New Spirit. "A new heart also will I give you, and a new spirit will I put within you: and I will take away the stony heart out of your flesh, and I will give you an heart of flesh," (Ezekiel 36:26).

Speak With New Tongues. "They shall speak with new tongues," is the promise of Mark 16:17.

Listen For New Instructions. "A new commandment I give unto you, That you love one another; as I have loved you, that ye also love one another," commanded Jesus in John 13:34.

Remember You Are A New Creature. "Therefore if any man be in Christ, he is a new creature: old things are passed away; behold, all things are become new," (2 Corinthians 5:17).

Put On The New Man. Paul encouraged us to "Put on the new man, which after God is created in righteousness and true holiness," (Ephesians 4:24).

Embrace The New Covenant. "In that he saith, A new covenant, he hath made the first old. Now that which decayeth and waxeth old is ready to vanish away," (Hebrews 8:13).

Remember His Promise Of A New Name. "Him that overcometh will I make a pillar in the temple of My God, and he shall go no more out: and I will write upon him the name of My God, and the name of the city of My God, which is new Jerusalem, which cometh down out of Heaven from My God: and I will write upon him My new name," (Revelation 3:12).

Let Him Make All Things New. "And He that sat upon the throne said, Behold, I make all things new. And He said unto me, Write: for these words are true and faithful," (Revelation 21:5).

Never doubt it. God changes the seasons of your life.

Appetites change.

Needs change.

Friendships change.

Goals change.

Your *dreams* change.

The location of your *home* changes.

This is what stands out remarkably in the life of the Moabite woman, Ruth.

Ruth cooperated with the changing of the seasons.

Every Friendship Nurtures
A Strength or
A Weakness.

-*MIKE MURDOCK*

～ 24 ～

THE UNFORGETTABLE WOMAN KNOWS A GOOD MAN WHEN SHE SEES ONE

Few do.

Frequently, I read a lot of magazines. Women's magazines are especially interesting as they reveal so much of the mindset of our present generation. The titles of articles are humorous, yet tragic. There is an overwhelming wail and lament rising from some women in America that they are abused, misused and falsely accused. The television talk shows are an hourly parade of emotional sewage as people spew out their fume, fury and failures.

"I always marry the wrong kind of man," wails one woman.

"He has beaten me for over 15 years," one sad-eyed victim whines.

If the guests who parade on our talk shows here in America are trophies of Mr. and Mrs. Average America, our whole world is in one sad, tragic predicament. We're always blaming our problems on everyone else...that *we have chosen to bond with!*

We choose a wife—and then proclaim to the world

that she is ignorant, insensitive and inattentive to our needs.

We choose a husband—and then complain that he's lazy, unaffectionate and unfaithful. Yet in a world of millions, *he was our number one choice to pour our life into!*

Somehow, it never occurs to us to assume the responsibility *of our choices*—to look into the mirror and admit that we are using the wrong criteria, if we keep on making the wrong choices.

▶ You Will Not Find Right People In The Wrong Places.

▶ You Will Not Find Good People In The Bad Places.

▶ You Will Not Find Pure People In Impure Places.

"Where did you meet your husband?" asked the television talk show host of a young woman complaining about her husband who was an alcoholic. "In the bar," was the reply.

That is why I admire Ruth. She found a good man, Boaz.

Here Are 27 Qualities of The Good Man Ruth Found

1. He *Worked*.
2. He Worked *Diligently*.
3. He Had Employees Working Under Him.
4. He Owned Land.
5. He Had His Own House.
6. He Was Known In The Community.
7. He Interrogated Others About Her.
8. His People Around Him Were Informed, Alert

And Aware of Who Ruth Was, Her Background And Her Work Style.

9. Those He Trusted Were Trustworthy.

10. He Knew And Discerned Her Difference.

11. He Gave Ruth Access To Him.

12. He Exposed Ruth To Those Closest To Him.

13. He Willingly Invited Her To Participate In The Circle of His Life.

14. He Was Not Afraid of Her Getting To Know More About Him And His Business.

15. He Was Gracious And Kind To Her.

16. He Took Steps To Prevent Others From Making Wrong Remarks About Her.

17. He Protected Her Purity And Focus.

18. He Instructed Those Around Him To Do Extra Things of Kindness Toward Her.

19. He Was Informed About Her Attitude, Compassion And Mercy Toward Naomi, Her Mother-In-Law.

20. He Knew Where She Came From.

21. He Was Aware of The Efforts And Difficulties She Was Willing To Go Through To Make Adjustments.

22. He Knew God Was Her Provider And Would "Recompense Thy Work, And A Full Reward Be Given Thee of The Lord God of Israel Under Whose Wings Thou Art Come To Trust."

23. He Honored The Fact That She Trusted God For Everything She Wanted, Instead of Begging Him To Pay Her Bills.

24. He Comforted Ruth.

25. He Spoke Friendly To Her, Even Though She Was A Foreigner.

26. Yet With All His Extra Blessing of Her, He

Never Demanded Anything of Her.

27. He Did Not Make A Pass. He did not come on to her.

These are some of the characteristics of a good man. Never forget this Powerful Wisdom Secret: *A Good Man Will Expect You To Trust Your God For Your Provision.*

The world system is different. Thousands of women live with men who will pay their bills, making them a servant to his provision. *Any man who does this has purchased you without the responsibility of being faithful to you.*

You see, a *godly man will want you to trust God.* This is not because he could not provide. Boaz was very capable and instructed them to leave handfuls on purpose for her. But there is never an end to your blessing and provision *if God is your source.*

Men die.

Your God is forever.

Men change.

Men quit.

Boaz was a godly man.

He met every criteria of a godly man.

Ruth knew an extraordinary man when she met him.

That's why she was an *Unforgettable Woman.*

≈ 25 ≈

The Unforgettable Woman Cooperates With The Local Customs And Protocol

It was the custom for a widow to marry the nearest kinsman, who could purchase the ground of her dead husband, and then perpetuate the Seed through children. Naomi gave Ruth that privilege by encouraging her to approach Boaz. And Ruth replied to Naomi, "All that thou sayest unto me I will do. And she went down unto the floor, and did according to all that her mother in law bade her," (Ruth 3:5-6).

Tradition contains limitations.

Custom is not *always* in the best interest in any locality.

Established protocol can be questioned.

However, there is great benefit in respecting authority. *Great favor flows when the rules of conduct are appreciated and respected.*

Most of us learn from books on etiquette, caring mothers and friends who reprove us when we get out of hand.

Acceptable rules of behavior are valuable. They bond people. They link people. They create the comfortable climate that launches friendships.

Relationships Are Strengthened Because of Protocol.

Ruth was from Moab. She was unfamiliar with the customs of Naomi's people. But she knew the incredible *rewards of cooperation.* Remember this.

The Unforgettable Woman Knows The Rewards of Cooperation.

Those who do not treasure the rewards of cooperation often wind up in prison or unemployed.

The purpose of authority is to create order.

Order Is Simply The Accurate Arrangement of Things.

The purpose of order is to *increase your productivity.*

Productivity determines your rewards.

This explains red lights and stop signs. It explains speed limits. Rules increase safety and the protection of us all.

Attend seminars, read books and listen to tapes that show you the rules of conduct and guidelines for social behavior with others.

3 Rewards of Honoring Protocol

▶ It will multiply your effectiveness in communication.
▶ It will increase your ability to make friends.
▶ It can reduce the number of enemies throughout your lifetime.

It is a Master Secret in the life of *The Unforgettable Woman.*

❧ 26 ❧

THE UNFORGETTABLE WOMAN IS WILLING TO MAKE ANY CHANGES NECESSARY FOR THE MAN IN HER LIFE

Ruth worked in the fields gathering barley or wheat, depending on the season. One day, she came home and was sitting there with Naomi. Her hair was probably matted, sweat pouring down her body. She was exhausted and worn out. Undoubtedly, she looked as bad as anyone could look at the end of a long, hard day!

Naomi gives her advice about approaching Boaz. "Now do what I tell you—bathe and put on some perfume and some nice clothes and go on down to the threshing-floor," (Ruth 3:3 LB).

Men respond to *sight*.

Women respond to *touch*.

I don't know all the details, but all of us will agree that men and women are totally different creatures.

Needs differ.

Tastes differ.

Hygiene matters.

Appearance matters.

Ruth packaged herself for where she was going, instead of where she had been.

The attire of a *harlot* is discussed in Proverbs 7.

The attire of a *virtuous woman* is discussed in Proverbs 31.

In Genesis, Joseph shaved his beard and changed his raiment because the Egyptians hated beards. He wanted to create a *climate of acceptance* in the palace of Pharaoh.

Even Timothy was instructed by the Apostle Paul on the appearance and clothing of women in the church.

I attended an amazing seminar some months ago. It was on appearance and how to create a sense of balance with clothing, even to changing the colors you were wearing.

Packaging Determines Desire.

Naomi was brilliant. She taught Ruth how to give Boaz a *picture he would want to remember.* A picture that gave him a *desire to reach.*

Some months ago, I was driving by a home. The wife was waving good-bye to her husband as he was backing out of the driveway. Her hair was in curlers. Her bathrobe looked torn, wrinkled and probably had a button or two missing. I wasn't close enough to smell her breath, but I certainly could imagine it! She was waving to him a good-bye and *giving him a permanent photograph of what was awaiting him upon his return home.* (Maybe that explained why he couldn't wait to get to work!)

I had to laugh inside. I could just imagine his thoughts of "home" as he drove by the billboards of beautiful ladies and walked into his office with everyone packaged nicely and attractively.

What am I saying? *You must make yourself desirable for the man you desire.*

The president of the largest employment agency in the world said that over 90 percent of the people who are hired were hired because of their *personal appearance.*

You are a walking message system. People *see* what you are *before they hear* what you are.

Imagine riding on an airplane and noticing that the pilot has catsup all over his shirt. Imagine his hair uncombed. Imagine dirt all over the bottom of his shoes. Now, try to imagine sitting in the seat and noticing torn seat covers on your seat. Several light bulbs are smashed. What is your next thought? "I wonder if anyone has *checked the engine?* I wonder if there is enough *fuel* in the tanks? I wonder if they have had the mechanics provide accurate maintenance?"

Packaging Determines Whether You Reach or Withdraw.

Look at the products you purchase at the store. *Everything* you are buying is based on...*appearance.*

Make any change necessary today that will make you more desirable to your man. It may be braces on your teeth, taking your clothes to the cleaners for pressing, or finding the lipstick with exactly the right color for you.

This kind of attitude made Ruth an *Unforgettable Woman.*

What Attracts
A Man's Attention
Does Not Always
Attract His Respect.

-MIKE MURDOCK

≈ 27 ≈

THE UNFORGETTABLE WOMAN IS ACCESSIBLE, AGREEABLE AND AGGRESSIVE

She was *accessible.*

Accessible means capable of being reached, used, seen or known: obtainable.

Visibility is a major factor in the currents of favor. Esther did not become queen until she was *seen.* When Jesus *saw* Zaccheus in the tree, he responded and went home with him. That's why the woman who had an issue of blood experienced her healing. She *pursued,* reached and crawled through the crowd to make the connection. David would never have sent for Abigail had he not *seen* her.

Ruth worked daily in the fields.

Servants *saw* her.

Boaz *saw* her.

Her labor was *known.*

Her work habits were commonly *observed* on a daily basis.

One of my close pastor friends in Montreal, Canada, shared an interesting insight with me a few weeks ago. As a single minister, he had asked the Lord to provide him with the right mate.

He said, "God gave me the perfect wife."

"How did you know she was perfect for you, just through dating her?"

"She worked in my office in ministry daily. She was on time every single morning. Her work was impeccable, and her attitude was so Christ-like. I saw her on a daily basis under the identical pressures that I experienced. I knew she was perfect for my lifestyle *because she was totally committed to my life-style before I ever began dating her.*"

That's why your obedience to The Holy Spirit is so vital to your happiness. When He speaks to you to move to a certain city, *do it.* When He speaks to you to apply for a job at a specific company, do it. When He confirms in your heart that a certain church should be your home church, and that the man of God in that place has been ordained to be your pastor, *attend and commit your life there.*

Admittedly, accessibility can become burdensome. *Wrong* people may reach for you. Demands on you are made unnecessarily.

Christian singles often complain that they "never meet anyone." Yet they stay home during Wednesday night church services. They rarely attend the great prayer and faith conferences.

How about *your* life?

Are you asking God to send you a mate who prays a lot, and yet you never attend prayer meeting at your own home church?

Are you asking God to send you someone knowledgeable in the Scriptures, yet you never attend the weekly Bible studies?

Are you asking God to send you someone who is a great worker and an achiever in the business world, yet you never attend a business seminar?

Ruth was *agreeable.*

Agreeable means pleasing, pleasant, ready to consent. It means harmonious. When Boaz instructed her to remain in his fields for gleaning, she did so. When Naomi told her to do the same, she did so.

When Naomi told her to go and meet Boaz at the threshing floor after spraying perfume and changing her clothes, the Scripture says, "All that thou sayest unto me I will do," (Ruth 3:5).

Many women think agreeableness is boring, that men love to be contradicted, confronted and challenged.

What Attracts A Man's Attention Does Not Always Attract His Respect.

What turns a man's *head,* does not always turn his *heart.*

What makes a man *look,* does not always make him *listen.*

What makes him *listen,* does not always make him *yearn.*

An agreeable spirit bonds you with those you love. It enables you to focus on the same things, move in the right direction and enjoy each other.

What is true fellowship?

Feet walking the same direction.

Hands reaching for the same thing.

Backs bearing the burden together.

Eyes looking the same direction.

Minds thinking the same thoughts.

Hearts beating together.

Certainly, there is a *time* for debate. Benefits exist

in the combat of presenting opposing views and offering options and alternatives. "Iron sharpeneth iron," (Proverbs 27:17). But your attitude and spirit of harmony will produce *a thousand more benefits* than any stubborn act of rebellion will ever produce.

Ruth was *aggressive.*

Aggressive means "marked by driving energy or initiative."

Ruth was aggressive when she *refused* to go back to her family in Moab when Naomi, her mother-in-law, insisted. Her face was set like a flint. She was determined.

She was aggressive in following Naomi back to Bethlehem.

She was aggressive when she approached the workers of Boaz and asked for permission to glean in the fields.

She was aggressive when Naomi sent her to Boaz to discuss the possibility of marriage.

You Have No Right To Anything You Have Not Pursued.

Jesus taught aggressiveness. "Ask, and it shall be given you; seek, and ye shall find; knock, and it shall be opened unto you: for everyone that asketh receiveth; and he that seeketh findeth; and to him that knocketh it shall be opened. Or what man is there of you, whom if his son ask bread, will he give him a stone? Or if he ask a fish, will he give him a serpent? If ye then, being evil, know how to give good gifts unto your children, how much more shall your Father which is in Heaven give good things to them that ask Him?" (Matthew 7:7-11).

The Proof of Desire Is Pursuit.

Men Rarely Reach For What They *Need,* But They Always Reach For What They Really *Want.*

Miracles do not go where they are *needed.* Miracles go where they are desired and *pursued.*

This explains the healing of the man let down through the roof in Jesus ministry. It explains why Jesus went home with Zaccheus. Zaccheus was aggressive. He climbed up in the tree to see Jesus.

It explains why the woman with the issue of blood received her healing, because she pressed through the crowd to touch the hem of His garment.

It explains why the blind man received his healing when he cried out, "Jesus, thou son of David, have mercy upon me."

Asking Is The Beginning of Receiving. Move toward your dreams today. Seize the day. Seize your daily appointments and agenda. Develop total *focus* on the desires of your heart. Do you want to be *healed?* Then don't study the options and alternatives. Give your entire faith toward the healing power of Jesus.

Do you want to be debt-free? Then refuse to adapt to lack and the spirit of poverty. Nurture the mindset of the prosperous.

There's a difference between being broke and being poor.

Being *broke* is not having enough money.

Being *poor* is not having enough motivation.

Being *broke* is a *season.*

Being *poor* is an *opinion.*

God responds to aggressive faith.

It makes you *unforgettable.*

The Right Thing Done
At The Wrong Time
Becomes The Wrong Thing.

-MIKE MURDOCK

❧ 28 ❧

THE UNFORGETTABLE WOMAN UNDERSTANDS TIMING, WORK SCHEDULES AND THE FOCUS OF HER MAN

When Naomi, the wise mother-in-law, instructed Ruth to approach Boaz, she said, "...but make not thyself known unto the man, until he shall have done eating and drinking. And it shall be, when he lieth down, that thou shalt mark the place where he shall lie, and thou shall go in, and uncover his feet, and lay thee down; he will tell thee what thou shalt *do*," (Ruth 3:3-4).

Boaz had toiled an entire day. He was tired. Exhausted. He was finishing up work at the threshing floor. That was not the right time to approach a man about a lifetime decision about marriage. *People rarely make good decisions when they are exhausted.*

Tired Eyes Rarely See A Good Future.

After he worked, he relaxed through eating and enjoying his great meal. He was unwinding, settling down and mentally and emotionally preparing for his next day. Naomi understood this. Very few younger women would have considered this. Ruth accepted her advice. She implemented it immediately.

It worked.

Boaz awakened in the middle of the night, noticed her and the conversation began. She had *not* broken his focus from his work. She *had* respected his time, schedule and what mattered to him.

He responded perfectly.

Many women never really grasp the importance of *timing* when conversing with their man.

I have seen it happen scores of times. A man comes home exhausted and tired from a long day at the office. Mentally, he has made hundreds of decisions within the last 12 hours. Emotionally, he is trying to gather energy for the entire week ahead. He is responsible for the bills, insurances, upkeep of the home, discipline of the children, dealing with legal problems and people on his job that are unproductive around him.

He falls back into his recliner with the remote control in his right hand. The television comes on. It is relaxing to him to watch the football game begin. What happens next is normal across America. His wife suddenly walks through the door. She sees him sitting there "doing nothing," and she has a hundred questions to dump on him.

She walks to the television. She turns it off. She looks at him and speaks, *"We've got to talk."*

Those are the dreaded words every man hates to hear. Boaz did not have to worry about that kind of woman.

Ruth had been advised wisely.

She had been sitting at the feet of her mentor.

She understood timing.

She knew the power of *respecting the focus* of her man.

Certainly, the argument could be made that men do not understand the timing in approaching their wives, also! The point is that Ruth had a quality every human needs: *Grasping the importance of timing,* the work schedules and the focus of others around us.

One day I was very intently writing a letter that required me to summon every ounce of understanding within me. Mentally, I shut everyone and everything out. My creative mind was birthing. My heart was pounding in an effort to communicate a specific truth in words on paper. Imparting invisible thoughts to others through writing can be exhausting and exhilarating at the same time.

Suddenly, the door opened. Someone walked in and yelled, "What do you want to eat?"

The magic of the moment splintered into pieces. The climate was shaken like an earthquake would shake California. I cannot count how many times that broken focus has robbed me of hundreds of perfect ideas being birthed within me by someone simply being thoughtless.

You have seen it happen when a mother suddenly saw her baby fall on the floor while driving. She reaches back to catch him. Her car crashes. Broken focus. Timing.

Have you ever been watching and listening carefully to a political debate on TV and had someone else begin discussing things with you without any regard whatsoever to your intense concentration? Have you ever been reading a book intently, and had someone break into your concentration with the most mundane and ridiculous questions or statements about things of no interest to you? Of course you have.

When you approach others who are deep in conversation, observe these two principles:

Allow others the privilege of finishing what they have started.

Learn to enter conversations at the right time with the right words.

The Unforgettable Woman understands the importance of timing.

❧ 29 ❧

THE UNFORGETTABLE WOMAN BUILDS A REPUTATION OF INTEGRITY, COMPASSION AND PURITY

Everyone knew about Ruth.

Boaz describes it this way, "It hath fully been shewed me, all that thou hast done unto thy mother in law since the death of thine husband: and how thou hast left thy father and thy mother, and the land of thy nativity, and art come unto a people which thou knewest not heretofore," (Ruth 2:11).

Later he spoke, "Blessed be thou of the Lord, my daughter: for thou hast shewed more kindness in the latter end than at the beginning, inasmuch as thou followedst not young men, whether poor or rich...for all the city of my people doth know that thou art a virtuous woman," (Ruth 3:10-11).

People talk. Good things and bad things. False accusations and accurate assessments.

People spoke well of her. Her sacrificial attitude and dedication to preserving and maintaining the life of her widowed mother-in-law was a known fact in the community. Obviously, she had not even dated or bonded with any of the young men in the city—rich or poor. Her total focus was on Naomi.

Productivity is a choice.

This had registered heavily in the heart and mind of Boaz who did not hesitate to respond to her pursuit of him.

Others should commend you. "Let another man praise thee, and not thine own mouth," (Proverbs 27:2).

Reputation is more powerful than money. "A good name is rather to be chosen than great riches," (Proverbs 22:1).

A good name is more magnetic than a strong fragrance. "A good name is better than precious ointment," (Ecclestiastes 7:1).

Several years ago, I arrived at the house of a young lady to take her to supper. As we were driving to the restaurant, she remarked: "I had another date planned tonight, but I told him I had to visit a relative in the hospital."

She had lied. It sickened me. I had been excited about establishing a relationship with her only to find out within minutes that falsehood came naturally and easily to her. Obviously, I would be the next victim on her list. It was the first and last date I had with her.

Whatever it takes, develop integrity.

Focus on it. Carefully examine each word and sentence that comes forth from your lips. Never say anything insincere. Refuse to brag on someone's singing if it is untrue. Don't say things merely to encourage others. "Recompense to no man evil for evil. Provide things honest in the sight of all men," (Romans 12:17).

The *compassion* of Ruth was known.

Observe how a woman speaks to her mother. Note

well how a man treats his mother. Also, observe how he reacts to the struggles and heartaches of the unfortunate.

Her purity and virtue were known. Admittedly, many false accusations are hurled these days. Good people have been stained through vindictive and violent people. Joseph is not the only story where someone who has walked totally before the Lord and has had his reputation devastated by those who had been refused or ignored.

However, the entire town knew of her obsession and kindness to her mother-in-law. *They said that she treated her mother-in-law better than 7 sons would treat a mother.* That kind of treatment is almost unheard of these days.

This doesn't mean you have to advertise all your good deeds. It is not important that you trumpet to the world all your acts of kindness and mercy. Somehow, God has a way of "letting it be made known."

What you are will eventually be exposed and known.

Yes, these are the marvelous qualities that make you *unforgettable.*

The Proof of Love
Is The Desire
To Protect.

-MIKE MURDOCK

≋ 30 ≋ *Naomi-mother in law*
Ruth - Daughter

THE UNFORGETTABLE WOMAN PROTECTS THE REPUTATION OF ANOTHER RATHER THAN DESTROYING IT

Ruth was a protector.

There's an interesting insight when Ruth approached Boaz in the middle of the night. He had told her, "Let it not be known that a woman came into the floor," (Ruth 3:14). He knew it would soil both their reputations if someone looked and saw her leaving in the morning hour. So, "she rose up before one could know another" and left before daybreak.

She could have had a photographer to photograph the occasion, or told her closest friends, or whatever. Not Ruth.

She honored his desire. *She was not uncooperative*
She understood it. *She didn't question the request*
She did not consider it rejection. *She knew it was his protection*
She saw his Wisdom. *And respected it.*
She wanted to protect his name as well as her own.
She was discreet. ~~not~~ *She didn't make herself noticeable*

Many women can be very vindictive. This is a

vindictive age. You read it in the paper every day. You watch it on television. Someone who feels scorned becomes consumed with revenge and retaliation. They are willing to forfeit everything they have built in their life to destroy someone who has hurt them.

No normal man would ever want to date a woman who sought to destroy another man. No man in his right mind would even want to date a woman who had sued another person in an effort to destroy them.

Discretion is a rare, remarkable and treasured quality.

Ruth had it.

It is what made her *unforgettable*.

≈ 31 ≈

The Unforgettable Woman Never Permits Her Past To Decide Her Future

Ruth created a future far different from her past.

Ruth was a Moabitess girl raised in heathenism. Moab was the son of incest between Lot and his daughter. She married Boaz, who one writer said had come through the loins of a temple prostitute by the name of Rahab. God put them together...and ushered in the lineage of Jesus Christ.

Ruth and Boaz produced Obed. Obed produced Jesse. Jesse produced David. David ushered in the lineage of Jesus Christ. Who was Ruth?

Ruth was the great-grandmother of David, the greatest warrior Israel had ever known. She was the great-great-grandmother of the wisest man who ever lived on earth, Solomon. Through her and Boaz came the precious son of the living God, Jesus of Nazareth.

God Never Consults Your Past To Decide Your Future. Satan may remind you of yesterday's mistakes. Don't listen to him. God never reads your diary. Your past is over. Act like it. Talk like it. Live like it.

Your best days are *ahead* of you.

Your worst days are *behind* you.

There Are 3 Kinds of People You Permit In Your Life

Today, Yesterday and Tomorrow People.

Those that God used yesterday may not have a single place in your future. Don't worry about it. Move quickly toward the promises of God. Prepare to enter your future without yesterday people.

You will not make the mistakes of yesterday again. *You have more knowledge today than you have ever had in your whole lifetime.* You have learned from the *pain.* You have learned from your *losses.* You have watched carefully and documented what's happened in other people's lives.

Do not fear that yesterday will crawl behind you like a predator and choke you to death.

It will not happen. "Remember ye not the former things, neither consider the things of old. Behold, I will do a new thing; now it shall spring forth; shall ye not know it? I will even make a way in the wilderness, and rivers in the desert," (Isaiah 43:18-19).

"Forgetting those things which are behind, and reaching forth unto those things which are before, I press toward the mark," (Philippians 3:13-14).

The Holy Spirit is your Enabler. "But ye shall receive power after that the Holy Ghost is come upon you," (Acts 1:8).

The Holy Spirit is your Comforter. "But when the Comforter is come, Whom I will send unto you from the Father, even the Spirit of truth," (John 15:26).

The Holy Spirit is your Teacher. "He shall teach

you all things, and bring all things to your remembrance, whatsoever I have said unto you," (John 14:26).

The Holy Spirit is the Revealer of those things which are to come. "Howbeit when He, the Spirit of truth, is come, He will guide you into all truth," (John 16:13).

As you pray this prayer with me, I ask The Holy Spirit to begin to dominate your mind and your life more than you have ever known...that He would consume you and that you develop a precious relationship with Him, knowing that yesterday is behind you, and the greatest days of your life are now being scheduled.

Our Prayer Together...

"Holy Spirit, I welcome You in my heart. In my home. In my life. I gladly submit to Your authority, Your plans and Your will for my life.

Teach me the ways of God. Teach me Your ways. I do not want to ever offend You, grieve You, or quench You in any way. Your Presence is my consuming desire. I long for Your constant approval. I am willing to be corrected, and I treasure Your voice within me. Yesterday is over, and from this day forward, You are my Authority, my constant Companion and the Comforter of my life. In Jesus' name. Amen."

DECISION PAGE

Will You Accept Jesus As Your Personal Savior Today?

The Bible says, "That if thou shalt confess with thy mouth the Lord Jesus, and shalt believe in thine heart that God hath raised Him from the dead, thou shalt be saved," (Romans 10:9).

Pray this prayer from your heart today!

"Dear Jesus, I believe that You died for me and rose again on the third day. I confess I am a sinner...I need Your love and forgiveness...Come into my heart. Forgive my sins. I receive Your eternal life. Confirm Your love by giving me peace, joy and supernatural love for others. Amen."

❑ Yes, Mike, I made a decision to accept Christ as my personal Savior today. Please send me my free gift of your book, *31 Keys to a New Beginning* to help me with my new life in Christ.

NAME _____ BIRTHDATE _____

ADDRESS _____

CITY _____ STATE ____ ZIP _____

PHONE _____ E-MAIL _____

Mail To:

The Wisdom Center · 4051 Denton Hwy. · Ft. Worth, TX 76117
1-817-759-BOOK · 1-817-759-2665 · 1-817-759-0300
You Will Love Our Website..! WisdomOnline.com

Clip and Mail

DR. MIKE MURDOCK

1 Has embraced his Assignment to Pursue...Proclaim...and Publish the Wisdom of God to help people achieve their dreams and goals.

2 Preached his first public sermon at the age of 8.

3 Preached his first evangelistic crusade at the age of 15.

4 Began full-time evangelism at the age of 19, which has continued since 1966.

5 Has traveled and spoken to more than 17,000 audiences in over 100 countries, including East and West Africa, Asia, Europe and South America.

6 Noted author of over 250 books, including best sellers, *Wisdom for Winning*, *Dream Seeds*, *The Double Diamond Principle*, *The Law of Recognition* and *The Holy Spirit Handbook*.

7 Created the popular *Topical Bible* series for Businessmen, Mothers, Fathers, Teenagers; *The One-Minute Pocket Bible* series, and *The Uncommon Life* series.

8 The Creator of The Master 7 Mentorship System, an Achievement Program for Believers.

9 Has composed thousands of songs such as "I Am Blessed," "You Can Make It," "God Rides On Wings of Love" and "Jesus, Just The Mention of Your Name," recorded by many gospel artists.

10 Is the Founder and Senior Pastor of The Wisdom Center, in Fort Worth, Texas...a Church with International Ministry around the world.

11 Host of *Wisdom Keys with Mike Murdock*, a weekly TV Program seen internationally.

12 Has appeared often on TBN, CBN, BET, Daystar, Inspirational Network, LeSea Broadcasting and other television network programs.

13 Has led over 3,000 to accept the call into full-time ministry.

THE MINISTRY

1 **Wisdom Books & Literature** - Over 250 best-selling Wisdom Books and 70 Teaching Tape Series.

2 **Church Crusades** - Multitudes are ministered to in crusades and seminars throughout America in "The Uncommon Wisdom Conferences." Known as a man who loves pastors, he has focused on church crusades for over 43 years.

3 **Music Ministry** - Millions have been blessed by the anointed songwriting and singing of Mike Murdock, who has made over 15 music albums and CDs available.

4 **Television** - *Wisdom Keys with Mike Murdock*, a nationally-syndicated weekly television program.

5 **The Wisdom Center** - The Church and Ministry Offices where Dr. Murdock speaks weekly on Wisdom for The Uncommon Life.

6 **Schools of The Holy Spirit** - Mike Murdock hosts Schools of The Holy Spirit in many churches to mentor believers on the Person and Companionship of The Holy Spirit.

7 **Schools of Wisdom** - In many major cities Mike Murdock hosts Schools of Wisdom for those who want personalized and advanced training for achieving "The Uncommon Dream."

8 **Missions Outreach** - Dr. Mike Murdock's overseas outreaches to over 100 countries have included crusades in East and West Africa, Asia, Europe and South America.

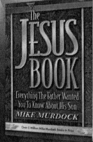

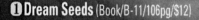

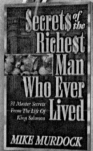

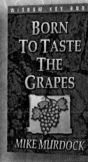

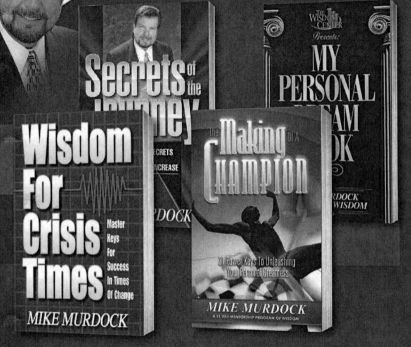